香港風俗
Hong Kong
Style

胡恩威
Mathias Woo

Mathias Woo

胡恩威

　　香港藝術家，於香港及倫敦修讀建築，從事劇本創作、劇場編導、多媒體及舞台設計、建築設計、藝術教育、文化政策評論等工作。

　　進念·二十面體聯合藝術總監暨行政總裁，從事編劇、導演、監製和策劃等工作，劇場作品逾六十齣，曾應邀於北京、南京、東京、新加坡、台北、柏林、布魯塞爾、波蘭等世界多地上演，主題涵蓋文學、歷史、時政、建築、宗教等，尤擅長運用多媒體科技從事舞台創作，作品包括《路易簡的時代和生活》、《萬曆十五年》、《華嚴經》、《東宮西宮》系列，及崑劇《臨川四夢湯顯祖》等。

　　著作包括《香港風格》系列 —《香港風格(2)—消滅香港》、《香港風格(3)—城市是應該這樣建成的》、《經濟危機 文化機遇？》及《香港的敵人是香港自己》。

　　此外，又為香港亞洲電視政治喜劇《東宮西宮TV》擔任監製、導演及編劇；並為亞視電視節目《我要做特首》任監製及主持。

Mathias Woo was born in Hong Kong, and he studied architectural design at the University of Hong Kong and the AA School of Architecture, London. He engages in theatre and multi-media creative works, architectural designs, and scriptwriting for both theatre and movies, and is well-versed in cultural policies and arts education.

Co-Artistic Director cum Executive Director of Zuni Icosahedron, Mathias Woo leads a career as a scriptwriter, director, producer as well as curator, and is recognised for a portfolio of more than 60 theatre works, which have been invited to stages in cities around the globe such as Beijing, Shanghai, Nanjing, Tokyo, Singapore, Taipei, Berlin, Brussels of Belgium and Krakow of Poland. Mathias' theatre works explore subjects as wide-range as literature, history, architecture, religion, current political affairs. His recent productions include 18 Springs, 1587: A Year of No Significance (an adaptation from historian Ray Huang's book of the same title), Hua-Yen Sutra, East Wing West Wing Series and Multimedia Architecture Music Theatre Series.

Mathias' publications consist of the Hong Kong Style Series, Cultural Opportunities in Economics Crisis, Hong Kong Is Its Own Enemy, to name a few.

During 2011 – 2012, Mathias made himself producer of TV talk shows I Want to Be Chief Executive and East Wing West Wing (TV version), and anchored for the former show.

目錄
Contents

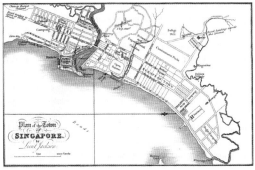

1828年的新加坡城市地圖 （圖片提供／陳家毅）
1828 Plan of Singapore Town Map (Image provided by Tan Kay Ngee)

為港把鏡，為加把勁

撰文：陳家毅

　　近幾年在新加坡，因為參與「馬來古區」百年老店屋的修繕工作，有機會接觸到古區的資料，追溯老宅的歷史。其中有張收藏在「新加坡文物局」的老地圖，描述了英國人在一八二八年，如何瞄準新加坡河優越的地理位置，在岸邊佈下了一局影響至今的城市棋盤。

　　手描的「市中心規劃圖」顯露了當年遠征者的野心。橫縱有序的大小街道將區域塊分出來：河嘴新設了行政區，面前有個草地廣場。背後的小山插上英國旗幟，是可瞭望南海的鎮守基地。植物公園、英歐區緊貼在行政廣場的北與東側。為方便殖民政府的控管，佔大多數人口的華族，巧妙的與本地馬來族隔離；至今不變的「牛車水」和「馬來區」原來一早就被分別安置在市地圖左右的兩端。

　　閉上眼睛片刻，相似的地圖浮現腦海：河嘴既是上海外灘、蘇州河，英、法租界同樣將中國人隔離開去；新加坡的規劃初稿，也是香港從中環水邊的兩旁延伸開去的殖民城市雛型。這或許就解釋了為甚麼多年來我對上海、香港這兩個城市雖認識不深，卻完全不感到陌生的奇異原因吧。

按部就班有條不紊的英國人，在亞洲，由西漸東，從南上北，而後又南下。三個海港城市日常生活的操作，至今仍然依循着當年留下的規格。快兩百年過去了，多少星遷月移物是人非，三個城市的居民添置、改造、修建、再規劃屬於他們自己的空間。三地人分別耕耘三幅田地，開出了不同的花，也結出不同的果實。

　　《香港風格》的讀者對象顯然是土生土長的香港人。胡恩威為忙碌的香港人把鏡，毫不遺留地照出城市自身的美與醜；匆忙間他們沒留意到隨時間流逝，身邊環境有了巨大的變化。建築物日漸密擠，街道上陽光日漸減少——現代亞洲人對「繁榮」的追求，導向普遍的誤思。全書由香港島先行探討，細細梳理至九龍半島。胡恩威的觀察精準入微，描述自己的城市愛惡分明。

　　每當初抵香港，我總被車窗外的連綿山脈和水色吸引，隨而取代的是連綿高樓，天然的壯觀令人為之屏息，瞬間卻變成了人工建物。三五天後更開始感覺到這城市自我給與的壓迫感。雖有海洋、公園、山林也難以覺察，因為早已被辦公或住宅大樓阻擋掩蓋掉了。

　　香港市景本來就像舞台上的帷幕拉開，是令人讚嘆的一台佈景，層次多姿又有景深。它的色彩累積了港人多年的喜好、習俗，還有中西不拘、雅俗共存的開放性，產生的是謂「風格」。可喜的是渾然而成的香港風格毫不造作，可惜的是民粹美學日漸消失。《香港風格》帶我們過街穿巷，從台前轉向佈景的背後，探尋這城市的框架和結構，從而引出經濟的、政治因素的叩問。

「風格」不過是種副產物，在香港尤其明顯地被發揚光大，民間的多元性為香港打開了新的可能性。無論是鬧哄哄龍蛇混雜的旺角，或隨街可見中西參半的「茶餐廳」，皆反映了香港人的機智和應變能力。像「鴛鴦」這道地飲料，原創者還需有自信、膽識，和一點幽默感才行！

這一點胡恩威明白，他更清楚地知道香港地理位置的優勢，但卻又很無奈——建築和城市被帶動的商業行為所操縱，快速的被蠶食；政府無策的失職，令他按捺不住，文字間流露一股氣怒。畢竟，再富有的資本城市，還需要超越民間的行政力量來導航；優質的未來生活才得以規劃，建築、街道、公園、廣場得以組織、維持與發展。否則，以利為先易的城市終會落得東湊西拼，甚至貧富縣殊的一個狀態。

胡恩威的文字保持他一貫的快捷敏思，閱讀過程常要來回翻對前章後段，讓人透視到他考慮事務的周詳與全面。我不禁暗想，他向來態度認真，對看不順眼的事情毫不留情直批，飯局間常常（對文化事尤其）「威」嚴發言，語氣懾人。背後往往又流露出他的懷舊，對鍾愛事物帶有某一種「溫柔」。而這「溫柔」，是他這位長年「黑衣人」所不太願意在人前顯露的，卻不經意地在字裡行間流露出來。也是全書最好看的地方。

因為他秉持的執著，所以「混凝土」或精緻稱呼的「清水泥」，在書中原汁原味保持為港所通用，外人看來也許覺得不甚文雅的「石屎」；同樣地「芬蘭浴」被拼成接近洋名原音的「桑拿」，「天花」為「樓底」等，港式中文的原創力，當然也是一種風格，油然浮現。

前半部多描述有趣味的城市角落和現象，後半部深進一步探究並討伐城市政策的缺失；也以比較灰喪、難以瞻望到美好遠景的筆調為全書結尾。令人掩卷深思，並且感慨胡恩威的孤立，和無助感。這也是外人所不太理解，為甚麼港人至今對自己的城市還未太能建立起「歸屬感」？為甚麼未能對生長的地方有着「家」的信念？至少在二零四六到來之前，除了保留難能可貴的自身風格，香港能夠做得更好更出眾的，應該還有許多許多。

二零一二年六月於DH

得獎無數的陳家毅建築師，1984年畢業於倫敦「建築聯盟」，1996年被日本《間》畫廊選為「世界581建築師」之一。著名的工程項目包括：曾獲威尼斯雙年展銀獅（群）獎的北京「長城腳下的公社」，2005年落成的「新加坡管理大學」，而今已成為城市著名景觀，以及2010年為國家設計「2010年上海世博會」的新加坡館。2012年擔任台灣「文化部」設計顧問，參與新標誌設計，和舊辦公大樓的空間改造。出版文集有《不完夢》（1978）、《重顧草莓地》（2006，2009），以及《城市磁場》（2008，2009）。

A Mirror and A Spur

Tan Kay Ngee

In recent years, due to my involvement in the restoration of Singapore's historical Malay Village, I found myself delving into archival materials regarding the heritage and history of local old houses. Amongst the materials was an ancient map I encountered at the National Heritage Board, describing how, in 1828, the British, noticing the geographical advantages of the Singapore River, placed a city on its banks – an important piece in the geopolitical game of chess even today.

The hand-drawn "City Centre Plan" still conveys the brash audacity of those early colonists. The orderly streets and byways were divided neatly into zones: on the prime land by the estuary sat the Governors' Quarters, facing a stately parade green field square. Behind the small hill on which the British flag flew, was the military garrison gazing out upon the southern Straits. The Botanical Gardens and European Quarters were located right next by, to the North and East of the Governors' Quarters. To facilitate the rule of the colonists, the majority Chinese immigrants were kept ingeniously separated from the local Malays on two ends of the settlement area. The original Chinatown and Kampong Glam (Malay Village) still survive today, with their borders being relics from this original town plan.

Closing my eyes, two more maps superimposed on the one before me: of Shanghai's Bund and the Suzhou River, in which the English and French concessions were whole other worlds from their Chinese subjects. The first draft of town planning for Singapore also recalls Hong Kong's Central, from which the city gradually spread along both ends of its waterfront. Perhaps this explains the sense of familiarity I experience when visiting Shanghai or Hong Kong, despite lacking a more intimate knowledge of these cities.

This pattern of English settlement has gradually given way to a more indigenous orderliness, moving from South to North, and then South again. The three port cities' daily rhythms still carry a faint echo of those ancient plans. It's been nearly two hundred years, people and goods have moved relentlessly through these spaces; all three cities have seen the ebb and flow of population, development, restoration, seen the establishment of their laws and customs. Three different peoples have cultivated three cities, which have seen the flowering and fruition of three unique cultures.

Hong Kong Style appeals particularly to the Hong Kong home grown population. Mathias Woo, a typical busy Hongkonger, holds up a mirror to his city, confronting both its beauty and its ugliness, focusing on the oft-overlooked details that escape one's notice in the daily grind, capturing the rapidly changing landscape. Buildings bristle, growing denser, sunlight rationed to a smaller sliver by the day, reflecting the modern Asian's endless quest for wealth and development, and the unknowing sacrifices it requires. This book focuses first on Hong Kong Island and then combs carefully through the alleys and byways of Kowloon, where Mathias' lens reveals the surprising and delicately observed facets of his city.

When travelling to Hong Kong, I am always captivated by the mountains and waterways, but these scenic views are progressively displaced by endless high-rise edifices. The grandeur of nature has increasingly given way to the man-made cityscape. Usually, after three or four days of staying in the city, I feel claustrophobic. The surrounding sea, the gardens, the still-untouched mountains go unnoticed, overshadowed by towering skyscrapers.

The Hong Kong cityscape is like a set piece which the stage curtains drop to reveal, drawing admiring gasps from the audience, its many facets and layers captivating the viewer. Its sights and sounds have entertained many a Hongkonger, its interlacing customs and rhythms drawn from both East and West, its character both traditional and cosmopolitan. It is these things, perhaps, that constitute the Hong Kong "Style" – a "Way of Life". The vitality of this way of life lies in its rawness but sadly, this uniquely Hong Kong essence is also rapidly vanishing. *Hong Kong Style* allows us to peep behind the curtain, to the backstage, as it were, of Hong Kong life, to better understand the structure and inner workings of this great city, most elusive of all, its economics, and politics.

"Style" is but a by-product, an identity that has been touted in Hong Kong for consumption. The diversity of its population is its real strength, giving rise to new opportunities. Whether it is the chaotic bustle of Mongkok, or the mixed East-West heritage of the of "cha chan teng" (literally tea restaurants, a kind of casual dining cafes common in Hong Kong that provide Cantonese style western food), these aspects of Hong Kong reflect the innovation and resilience of native Hong Kongers. Even the "Mandarin Duck" （鴛鴦）, a staple beverage (coffee mixing with tea) in Hong Kong, also reflects the confidence, daring, and humour of its original creator!

Mathias Woo understands this, and even more, he understands the importance of Hong Kong's geographical heritage, and its inherent limitations – the architectural development of the city has been allowed to be controlled by the commercial interests that created it. In the absence of a strong administrative force, this insatiable commercial activity has been allowed to dominate the fabric of society, encroaching upon older ways of life. It is precisely this frustrates the author, an anger somehow shown between the lines. In the face of overwhelming vested interests and free-wheeling capitalism, it is even more critical the common folk have a countervailing force in the government to help navigate future development; Only in this way can lives be orderly; buildings, streets, gardens and public spaces be organised, maintained, and developed. The increasingly venal way of life will only make Hong Kong rootless, part of neither east nor west – the city may have grown economically, but at the expense of something more essential, as the rich get richer while the poor get poorer.

Mathias Woo's quick and sensitive prose requires close reading and rereading, in order to better grasp the subtleties and comprehensiveness of his thought. I can't help thinking that, due to his earnestness, he is quick to criticise and seldom minces his words, particularly when commenting upon art and culture. His strong words can seem startling at times. On the other hand, his writing is also steeped in nostalgia, and the things he loves he bathes in a glowing tenderness. Perhaps this "Man in Black" is reluctant to reveal this tender side, but his words betray him. And it is in these tender moments that the text truly moves the reader.

Holding on to his Hong Kong colloquial language, Mathias uses the more unrefined Cantonese term "stone shit" （石屎） repeatedly in the text for concrete, instead of "reinforced concrete" （混凝土）, or the more delicate "clear water mud" （清水泥）, even if outsiders might find the term not very decent. Similarly, the term "song-naa" （桑拿）, a phonetic translation of "sauna", has been used instead of the more literary "Finland bath" （芬蘭浴）, and "beneath the storey" （樓底） instead of "ceiling" （天花） etc, in order to retain the Hong Kong style vernacular.

The first half of the text focuses more on the hidden corners of the city and the surprises they contain, whereas the second half dwells more seriously on the city's social policies and its defects; it is perhaps also the more pessimistic half, and the book ends on a rather gloomy note. It is a thought-provoking work, and leads one to lament the solitude of the likes of Mathias Woo, to lament his helplessness to effect change. This is also something that outsiders cannot understand, why do Hongkongers fail to greet their city with a sense of homecoming? Why do they lack a sense of belonging, a sense of home? Perhaps by the year 2046 at least, aside from preserving its unique style, there is still much more Hong Kong could achieve and excel – greater success and extensive progress. Indeed, a lot more.

June 2012 at DH

Tan Kay Ngee is an award-winning architect. He graduated from the Architectural Association, London in 1984 and was selected as one of the "581 World Architects" by Ma Gallery Tokyo in 1996. Projects of the office include: the Commune by the Great Wall in Beijing which won the Venice Biennale Silver Award in 2002, the Singapore Management University, and the Singapore Pavilion of Shanghai Expo 2010. He wss the design Consultant for Ministry of Culture, Taiwan in 2012, which involved in the designing of a new logo, and the renovation of the bureau. Collection of essays published include: "Never Ending Summer" (1978), "Strawberry Fields Revisited" (2006, 2009) and "Magnetic Fields of Cities" (2008,2009).

建築就是政治

撰文：胡恩威

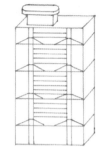

　　香港回歸前後，政府已經啟動了一系列消滅香港街道架構的政策，由舊區重建以至新型公共屋邨和新市鎮的規劃，都是把街道消滅或邊緣化的過程。舊區重建政策尤其嚴重，近十五年來的舊區重建發展都是把原有的小街小路和市集變為巨型太空船式的規劃，把小區的風味和風情都消滅了，囍帖街就是經典例子。其實過去二十年香港的土地規劃政策有一個最大的目標，就是把土地業權集中在港鐵和超巨型地產發展商身上，舊區重建就是把小業主小商戶的業權收回，重新分配給大型地產商，推行活化工廈及強拍也是以收業權為目標。香港政府是世界唯一一個自稱為國際城市的政府，卻作出這種不符合國際城市多元城市空間發展的土地政策。紐約倫敦巴黎東京等國際大都會，都非常重視街道的保育，以及中小型業主業權的保護。居者有其屋，商者有其舖，香港也是唯一一個沒有保護中小企業權政策的城市，沒有租管，沒有小業主權原區安置。

　　這些不合理的政策在九七前已經啟動，只是九七後沒有好好的去更正和修訂。香港原有的多元都市空間被破壞得特別厲害，近年自由行產生的問題，商業區商舖類型單一化，大集團獨大的情況，完全是政府缺乏規劃政策所致，美其名為市場主導，實際上是大財團主導，小商戶根本沒有能力在這種市場生存下來，而小商戶和小街小路正正是香港風格之所在。天星、皇后引起的保育問題被異化為單一的建築物保育，而不是香港城市空間和多元文化之保育，香港現在最需要保育的，是舊區的小街架構以及多元的小商戶文化，但香港政府並沒有進行任何有系統和具深度的研究，一切都是以大型商場地產發展為本。紐約倫敦的政府近年均大力推動街道保育，並進行系統性的街道生態研究，街道作為公共空間和社區空間的各種可能，街道與步行和騎單車等環保交通觀念的系統發展，香港在這方面的研究是十分欠缺的。運輸署只把單車當作運動休閒活動，而不是一種可能的交通工具。

　　所以我們今天要保衛的，是香港的街道，是香港的小業主業權，是香港人多元生活空間：小販、排擋、小店、民居。香港人不需要豪華會所，香港人需要更有人情味的生活空間、居住空間。可以漫步的街道空間，可以讓大家呼吸的生活休閒空間，小小的茶室咖啡書店士多。大型發展和小商戶是可以共榮共存的，東京就是好例子，為甚麼香港不可以？問題的核心是負責香港規劃政策的官員沒有人文精神，沒有規劃知識的深度培育，一切只以大型地產發展出發，而大型地產發展也可以容許「小」的存在，其實旺角的朗豪坊便是很好的一個實驗，但這種大中有小的實驗，好像沒有被進一步發展下去，香港舊區最寶貴的就是那些小街，把小街拿走，就是把香港的精神消滅。

　　香港建築師在香港缺乏影響力也缺乏發言權，造成這個原因，一方面是香港建築師學會過分封閉和自我保護，另一方面是香港建築師在大型發展項目下，根本沒甚麼重要角色可言。老實說，如果明天香港所有建築師都消失，對香港也沒有甚麼影響，但是律師、醫生、會計師消失，香港的運作一定會受到很大的影響。這是我們需要思考的，為甚麼其他國際大城市均十分重視建築師，香港卻越來越不重視。香港有的公司只是 Norman Foster，只可以是 Norman Foster，香港沒有好好去培育自身的建築師，香港建築師也沒有團結起來去爭取，香港的精英階層對建築師也沒有甚麼要求，香港最後一幢世界級建築已是八十年代的匯豐銀行和中國銀行大廈了。建築不重視創新與實用，空間只是一種投資的資產，而不是作為生活和創新的空間，這是香港目前面對的困局，也是建築的困局。

建築與城市規劃的模式和價值，反映了當權者的文化水平，民主不一定是有文化，獨裁也不一定是沒文化，新加坡李光耀在七十年代已經在規劃上從文化歷史角度保留新加坡舊區的小街架構以及傳統建築群，馬拉區、唐人街、印度區均被保留和活化。新加坡的小商戶也有足夠的生存空間，人民也是在合理的空間下生活與成家立業。香港自稱是自由之城，但在空間上，香港人卻漸漸失去自由發展的空間。香港人有批評任何人的自由，但沒有規劃自身空間的自由，政府官僚系統沒文化沒知識，只有程序和冷血的所謂公平公開制度，「以人為本」已經變了沒有任何意義的四字詞了。

政治是虛的，政策是實的，以人為本是政治術語的虛，沒有真實的以人為本政策，以人為本就好像為人民服務一樣，是太虛幻的政治迷藥。所以有文化有學識的民主才是真正的民主，才是真正的自由，香港現在的自由只是建立在虛幻的世界裡。唯有出現真正的空間和改變規劃政策，香港人才可以有真正的自由。規劃署的官員要變得更有學問，政府高官要更有學術文化知識和方法，香港人要有上進學習之心，要學會更多建築的知識以及更文明的爭取方法。建築和規劃是政治遊戲的產物，也說明了政治質素的高低。

　　香港是一個富有但沒有文化的社會？香港是一個財政上富有但精神文化貧乏的社會？日本近二十年經濟沒有快速發展，但空間建築是走向更樸實和多元的模式，年輕一代的建築師不是追求「豪華」和所謂「日本性」，而是以環保和社會角度發展不同類型的建築空間美學。日本的簡約美學也不是只有一種簡約美學，而是多元的，像中村好文的住宅設計，Bow wow、SANAA 和 TOYO ITO 的空間美學，更是具備人文情懷與文化實質的作品。

　　香港精英追求的豪，是物料上的豪，價錢上的貴，而不是文化上的樸實和品味的追求。香港風格原有的多元美學和品味，近二十年來被單一化、被低俗化了，豪宅就是一種今天非常香港的類型和風格。假西方高貴的宣傳廣告，偽水晶西方假豪宅樣式，大量的名貴雲石和高級廚房用具，豪華會所等等假大空，說明了香港這個時代的下流。財富是有了，但品味和品德都沒有了，一百年後的香港會是怎樣的呢？五百年後的香港又會變成怎樣呢？那些石屎高樓，那些雲石，那些亮光，都會成為怎樣的一種風景？香港遲早有一天會變成了一個廢墟？五百年後一千年後一萬年後？也許人類不再存在了。這樣的一種沒有品德和品味的資本主義社會，人變成了一種只有慾望的動物，建築也變得毫無空間可言，香港就是變成了這樣的一種都市，一個沒有人情沒有思想沒有文化沒有深度的低俗消費性城市了。目前香港政府的規劃政策和架構，只是單從金錢和經濟效益和行政效率處理規劃問題，建築在這種意識形態的規劃觀下，也只可以是紙上談兵式的規劃，而不是更多樣性的社會和文化價值規劃。

　　香港目前最嚴重的問題是沒有一個全面和具體深度的規劃研究和規劃決策系統，城規會那種委員會式的規劃決策只可以是決策過程的其中一個部分，而不應該是全部。運輸和規劃兩頭馬車各自規劃，也是十分奇怪。運輸署和規劃署的對等形式，也形成了香港一種只求交通效率，沒有社區交通規劃的模式。單車本來是十分有效的社區交通網絡，但在香港只被定位為消閒活動，原因是負責交通的運輸署只把車當作運輸工具。除了單車，小販和排擋也是香港政府取之而後快的香港傳統。這個殖民地設計出來的香港政府，本身就是要把香港消滅，把香港風格消滅，單車、小販、排擋、小店、民居，都是香港政府的消滅對象，所以香港的規劃政策模式都是以大商場、中央控制式的太空船堡壘架構為本來規劃。新區都沒有街沒有社區沒有生活空間，只有更大型的會所，更大型的中央冷氣商場，更大型的控制和更多的控制。香港已經越來越沒有都會的特色和自身的生活了，所以每逢假日，大量香港人，尤其是中產，均逃離到其他城市旅遊。台北、上海、東京、首爾，為的是尋找香港沒有的生活感。香港已經失去了太多的生活空間，街邊小販，大電影院，小店小舖，百貨公司，士多，文具店，玩具店，街頭叫賣，前舖後居，香港人越住越細，沒有社區空間，政客和官員只會口中說以人為本，實質是以自身利益為本。香港建築師也十分墮落，一切都是向錢看，沒有以建築知識積極參與香港規劃的時論和研究。墮落下去，是因為香港人殖民地移民心態的犬儒本質嗎？

Architecture is Politics

Mathias Woo

Since before the handover of Hong Kong, the government has been adopting a series of policies trying to destroy the street structure of Hong Kong. From the urban renewal plans to the building of new public housing estates and new towns, they are all part of the process of eradicating or marginalising streets and roads in Hong Kong. The situation is particularly severe in the urban renewal programme. In the last 15 years, the redevelopment programmes have been turning small streets and markets into projects like giant spaceships, wiping out all styles and flavours of small communities, and Lee Tung Street (commonly known as Wedding Card Street) is a typical example. In fact, in the past two decades, the major goal of Hong Kong's land use policy is to place all land ownership in the hands of MTR and some mega property developers. Urban renewal is a programme of recovering ownership of small businesses and reassigning it to large developers; and the purpose of revitalising industrial buildings and the land ordinance of compulsory sale for redevelopment is the acquisition of ownership. The Hong Kong Government is claiming itself to be the government of an international city, but it is the only government in the world to implement such a land use policy that is so contrary to the idea of diverse spatial development of an international city. Cosmopolitan cities like New York, London, Paris

and Tokyo make great effort in the conservation of streets and the protection of small property owners. Every person should have a house, and every trader should have a shop. Hong Kong is the only city with no policy protecting the rights of small property owners, and there is no rent control and no rehousing in the same district for small property owners.

This kind of unreasonable policies was adopted before the handover, but no one tried to correct or revise them after 1997. The versatile urban spaces of Hong Kong were destroyed, and the problem has been particularly severe in recent years with the launching of the individual visit scheme for people from the mainland. These years, shops in commercial districts are selling the same products catered for tourists from the mainland, and there is a growth in the dominance of large business groups. These problems are caused by the lack of planning and policies on the part of the government. They try to make things look nicer by saying we should have a market-oriented business model, but actually our market has become a domain ruled by large consortia where small businesses simply could not survive. However, the charm of Hong Kong style lies exactly in small streets and small roads with small shops. The issue of conservation as seen in the conflicts over the demolitions of Star Ferry and Queen's Pier is simplified into struggles for the preservation of individual structures, and not an issue of conservation of the diversity of Hong Kong's urban spaces. What we need to do now is to preserve the street structure of old districts and the pluralistic culture of small businesses in those areas. Nonetheless, the Hong Kong government did not conduct any systematic and thorough research on this, and let everything run in a business model with big shopping malls and real estate development as base. In recent years, street conservation has been vigorously promoted in New York City and London, and systematic studies of the ecology of streets have been carried out. These studies include the possibilities of developing streets as public and urban spaces, developing environmental traffic systems with streets for pedestrians only and cycling. Hong Kong lacks this kind of research, and the Transport Department takes cycling only as a sport or recreational activity, and never as a means of transport.

Thus, what we have to protect now are the streets and small property owners, as well as the pluralistic living spaces of Hong Kong, including hawkers, street food stalls, small shops and small houses. Hong Kong people do not need luxurious clubhouses, they need apartments and living spaces with human touches, streets where they could take a stroll, leisure and living spaces where they could breathe, like small cafés, small bookshops and grocery stores. Big development projects and small shops could coexist with mutual prosperity, and Tokyo is a good example. Why can't we do that in Hong Kong? The problem lies in the fact that the officials responsible for planning policies in Hong Kong do not have any cultivation in humanistic spirit, and they have very little training in urban planning, focusing only on large-scale property development. Little do they know that big real estate development plans could also accommodate small projects. Langham Place in Mongkok is one good example of the experiment of "big accommodating small", but it seems this experiment is not being further developed. What is most precious in the old districts are the small streets, and if they were taken away, the spirit of Hong Kong would be destroyed.

In Hong Kong, architects do not have much say and much influence, and the reason for this is because the Hong Kong Institute of Architects is too unreceptive and self-protective. At the same time, architects could never have any important role to play in large-scale development projects. Frankly speaking, if all architects in Hong Kong were to disappear tomorrow, it would create very little impact on Hong Kong; but if all lawyers, doctors and accountants were to disappear, there would be great consequences in our daily operation. This is something we need to think about. Why do other international cities attach so much importance on architects, while in Hong Kong architects are valued less and less? What we have in Hong Kong now is Norman Foster, and only Norman Foster. We are not nurturing architects of our own, and the local architects are not uniting up to fight. The elites in Hong Kong do not expect much from our architects, and the last world-class structures are the HSBC Building and Bank of China Tower built in the 1980's. Innovation and practical use are no longer important aspects in architecture now, and spaces are only assets for investment, and not spaces for living or creativity. This is the dilemma Hong Kong is facing, and also the dilemma of architecture here.

The model and value of architecture and urban planning of a city reflect the cultural level of the people in power. Democracy does not necessarily mean culture, and dictatorship does not necessarily mean the lack of culture. In the 1970's, Lee Kuan Yew, the prime minister of Singapore then, had already started to make plans for conservation of street structure and traditional buildings in old districts from the perspective of preserving cultural history. Conservation and revitalising plans were drawn and carried out in the Malaysian community, Chinatown and the Indian district. Small businesses in Singapore could make a reasonable living, and people there could have a reasonable space to enjoy their lives and start a family. Hong Kong calls itself a free city, yet in terms of space, Hong Kong people are losing their freedom for development. In Hong Kong, people have the freedom to criticise, but not the freedom to plan for their own space. The bureaucratic system here lacks culture and knowledge, and what we have are procedures and the cold-blooded so-called fair and open systems, and the term "human-oriented" doesn't mean anything anymore.

Politics is unreal while policies are real; human-oriented is virtual terminology when there are no human-based policies. In that case, the term human-oriented is just like the phrase "serve the people", an unreal political acid trip. Thus, only democracy with culture and knowledge is real democracy, and real freedom. The kind of freedom in Hong Kong is illusionary like a mirage. Only when there are real spaces and changes in the urban planning policies, could the people in Hong Kong enjoy real freedom. The officials in the Planning Department need to be more equipped with knowledge; high officials of the government should acquire more academic and cultural knowledge and be more resourceful; and people in Hong Kong should be more motivated in learning – to be more well-read in architecture and more civilised in their ways to fight for what they want. Architecture and urban planning are products of political games, and they also illustrate the quality levels of our politics.

Is Hong Kong a rich society with no culture? Is Hong Kong a rich society financially but poor spiritually and culturally? The economy of Japan did not have a rapid development in the last two decades, and their architectural spaces have been adopting a simpler and more diverse model. Young architects of the new generation there do not pursue after "luxurious" or the so called "Japanese" styles, but rather adopt a different set of aesthetics with different kinds of architectural spaces developed from various social and environmental points of view. The minimalist aesthetics of Japan is not just one strict set of aesthetics, it is diverse and versatile, such as the residential designs of Nakamura Yoshifumi, the works of Atelier Bow-Wow, SANAA and Toyo Ito. Their aesthetics of space and architecture is full of human touches and sentiments with cultural substances.

The kind of luxury that the elites of Hong Kong seek after is materialistic luxury in high prices, and they are not in pursuit of plain and honest taste in culture. In the last two decades, the diverse aesthetics and flavours of Hong Kong style have been homogenised and vulgarised; and luxury apartments are the typical Hong Kong style today. Advertisements of pseudo western grandeur, fake crystals, and phony luxury houses with lots of expensive marble and high-end kitchen appliances, and opulent clubhouse – all these illustrate the vulgarity and degeneration of our times. We have wealth, but no refinement and moral character. What would become of Hong Kong in a hundred years? What would become of Hong Kong in five hundred years? What would become of those concrete towers, the marble stones and the dazzling brightness ? What would it look like? Will Hong Kong turn into a ruin one day ? In five hundred years, one thousand years or ten thousand years? Perhaps, mankind no longer exists then. In such a capitalist society without refinement and moral character, men would become beasts of desire, and there would be no space for architecture. That is what is happening to Hong Kong now. It has turned into a city without human sentiments, without thoughts, without culture, without depth – a city of vulgar consumerism. At the present, the structure and policies for urban planning are drawn solely from the perspectives of money, economic and administrative efficiency. Under such ideology, architecture could only become idle theorising rather than pluralistic planning for social and cultural values.

The most serious problem in Hong Kong now is the lack of a comprehensive, specific and in-depth study on urban planning, as well as the absence of a policy making system. The Town Planning Board is operating like a committee in making plans and decisions, and this could work only if it is part of the policy making process and not the whole. It is quite odd that transport and urban planning are working separately. The way the Transport Department and the Town Planning Board are operating now under different umbrellas could lead only to traffic efficiency, what we have in Hong Kong now, without any transport planning model for the community. Cycling could be a very effective community transport mode, but in Hong Kong it is treated only as a leisure activity because the Transport Department considers cars to be the only means of transport on the road. Other than cycling as a mode of transport, hawkers and street food stalls are also Hong Kong traditions the government would like to get rid of. The aim of the Hong Kong Government is to destroy Hong Kong, to eradicate Hong Kong style. Bicycles, hawkers, street food stalls, small shops, small houses are all targets for elimination for the Hong Kong Government. Thus, models for urban planning in Hong Kong are big shopping malls, structures like space fortresses with central control systems. New towns have no streets, no communities, and no living space; all they have are large clubhouses, and larger shopping malls with central air-conditioning, larger and more control systems. Hong Kong has less and less cosmopolitan characteristics and individual lifestyles, and so on holidays and weekends a large number of Hong Kong people, especially the middle class, would escape to other cities like Taipei, Shanghai, Tokyo and Seoul for a trip, in order to look for a sense of life that is lacking in Hong Kong.

Hong Kong has lost too much living space already – hawkers, large cinemas, small shops, department stores, grocery stores, stationery shops, toy stores, street vendors, and shop-houses. The apartments of Hong Kong people are getting smaller and smaller, and there is no community space. "Human oriented" are only empty promises made by politicians and officials, and in reality everything they do is self-interest oriented. Architects in Hong Kong have become degenerates, working only for money, and reluctant to participate with their knowledge of architecture in the planning of Hong Kong or any research. Is it because of the cynical mentality of Hong Kong people as colonial immigrants that we have sunk so low?

石屎森林的美夢與夢魘
The Heaven and Hell of
Concrete Jungles

從山頂走下來
»A Stroll Downtown from Victoria Peak«

很多人都說香港地少人多，加上都市發展
快速，到處是石屎森林，沒甚麼看頭。
Many would describe Hong Kong as small and
packed. Under ultra-speed urban development, the
city is saturated as a concrete jungle, therefore without
much worth seeing.

我不同意，其實只要我們觀察身邊每一
個場景 ，不同時刻都會有不同體會。
I do not agree, only if we try to observe each and every
sight along our way, there could be a colourful variation
of experiences at different times.

而且，總要珍惜快將消失的過去。這次
從山頂走下來，重溫香港的自然和古調。
Moreover, the vanishing past is always treasured the
most. This walk down the Peak is to revisit the natural
and quaint Hong Kong.

香港的11月是秋高氣爽最宜散步的好季
節。氣溫適中，日光溫和而明亮，登高
行山最好。
In Hong Kong, November is the best time for taking
a stroll. The weather is mild, the sun is bright but soft,
nothing is better than a hike.

香港的山很多，在山上看香港，很立體很美麗。港島的山頂本身就是一座超級摩天大廈，在山頂不同的位置不同的季節不同的時分，可以看見不一樣的風景。夏天下大雨時看香港的大樓森林，都是灰灰的，像正在溶化；春天有點霧時，山頂的綠特別明顯；秋天時看則最立體，當陽光不太強烈時，可看到很遠的九龍半島。

There are a lot of mountains in Hong Kong. When viewed from the top, this city is very beautiful and three-dimensional. The mountaintop of Hong Kong Island itself is a super-tower. There is a diversity of sceneries in different parts of the peak, during different seasons or time of the day. When observed in a summer rainy day, the jungle of buildings in Hong Kong seems to be covered with a coat of grey and the buildings look like they are melting. In springtime with thin fog, the greens on the mountaintop are illuminated. The view in autumn is the most defined, when the sun is not too intense, one can see as far as the Kowloon peninsula.

這種古意盎然的石凳和林蔭，在香港已買少見少。 *This kind of quaint stone benches and tree shades are becoming rare in Hong Kong these days.*

在山頂走一個圈，看看香港島不同地區的變化，從中環到銅鑼灣灣仔西環、港仔薄扶林、甚至遠看九龍的獅子山。 *Taking a stroll around the Peak, watching the changes in different areas of Hong Kong Island, from Central to Causeway Bay, from Wanchai to the West, and from Aberdeen to Pokfulam, and even further to the Lion Rock in Kowloon.*

把老襯亭拆掉，換來不三不四的商場，是山頂大煞風景之作。 The Peak Tower was demolished and replaced by a strange looking and out-of-place shopping mall. The ambience of the old days is gone and it totally ruins the look of the Peak.

山頂凌霄閣：香港港島山頂道128號
The Peak Tower：128 Peak Rd, The Peak, Hong Kong Island

山頂是香港的發源地，早期是英國人聚居的地方。仍然保留很多殖民地時期的大屋和小路。不過，近十年來山頂的變化也很大。老襯亭拆了，新建了一個不三不四的商場，旁邊是另一個商場，白白浪費了山頂這個鳥瞰香港的好地方。以前的山頂餐廳是很有個人風格的老餐廳，政府為了錢，把地方租給另外一家公司，從前的感覺沒有了，代之而來的是一種扮中產的中庸氣氛，食物也造作了。

The city of Hong Kong first developed around Victoria Peak in its early days, as a British settlement. A lot of mansions and small paths from colonial time are still preserved. However, there were also some big changes in that area during the last decade. The Peak Tower was demolished and replaced by a strange and out-of-place shopping mall, with another mall aside, spoiling the best spot for a panoramic view of Hong Kong. In the old days the Peak Restaurant was an establishment with a strong identity, however, the government rents it out to a corporation for profit now, and the ambience of the old days is gone, instead, it becomes a place with a mediocre fake middle-class atmosphere, and the food is pretentious.

在山頂走路很愉快。清晨在山頂走一個圈，看着太陽慢慢升起，邊走邊看香港島不同地區的變化，中環銅鑼灣仔西環，香港仔薄扶林，甚至遠看九龍的獅子山。沿路有樹木、有天橋，時明時暗，像在半空中飛，小路旁還有些小屋小徑，很多都一直見證殖民地歷史。

Walking about the Peak is a very pleasant thing. One can take an early-morning stroll around the Peak to watch the sunrise and the variance of different areas of the Hong Kong island: Central - Causeway Bay - Wan Chai - Western District; Aberdeen and Pokfulam; even further to the Lion Rock in Kowloon. Along the way there are trees and bridges, sometimes bright and other times shaded, they seem to be floating in the air. On both sides of the roads are some small houses and paths; many of them have witnessed the Colonial history of Hong Kong.

山頂這一個圈下山的路，一條通往薄扶林水塘，另一條通往中環。通往中環的那條路，兩旁都種滿了老大樹，所以雖然路特別斜，上山下山很費力，但在夏天也會感到涼快。路上的街燈、路旁的長鐵木凳、秋天獨有的大樹芳香、落葉的香氣和顏色⋯⋯都是山頂才有的情景。走在薄扶林水塘的那條路，像到了郊外，間或看到高樓，但仍是郊野景色為主，走到盡頭就是香港大學師生的宿舍，而大學堂的老建築，更是各種傳統和鬼故事的靈感。

On this downhill route from the Peak, there is one path leading to Pokfulam reservoir and another leading to Central. The one to Central is lined with big ancient trees, although the path is steep and is not an easy hike, however, one would still feel cool and pleasant strolling there. The street lamps, the wood-and-iron benches, the special aroma from the woods that could be enjoyed only in autumn, the smell and colours of falling leaves ... all these are elements and images unique to the Peak. If one takes the path towards Pokfulam, it is like being in the country; perhaps you would spot a tall building or two, but natural landscape still dominates. At the end of the path are the student and faculty dormitories of Hong Kong University, the old structures that have inspired many traditional folk tales and urban legends.

沿着薄扶林道走到山道，是香港十大奇景之一，兩旁是高樓，中間架了一條斜斜的天橋，神功戲流行時，戲班就是在橋底的竹棚演出。山道下面是西環，雖然橋底下的中國國貨公司變了很多，以前的老店和茶樓買少見少，但西環仍保持一種歷史的魅力、一種老香港的感覺。沿着皇后大道西散步到中環，我知道沿途的街景很快就會消失，一有空就要到那裡走走，用相機拍下那些舊洋服店、涼茶舖、山貨店⋯⋯

Going through Pokfulam Road to Hill Road is one of the ten wonders of Hong Kong. There are tall towers on both sides, with a slightly inclined bridge in the middle. In the days when god-worshipping plays of Cantonese opera were popular, they were performed by troupes in a temporary bamboo shed theatre right underneath the bridge. Below Hill Road is the Western District (Sai Wan), although the Chinese products department store under the bridge has changed a lot and the old shops and tea houses are disappearing, the Western District has kept its historical charm and the impression of old Hong Kong. I can tell that many of these streetscapes along

山道的天橋，可以說是香港十大奇觀之一，也是一件解構主義建築品。
The flyover in Hill Road is really one of the Ten Wonders of Hong Kong. It is like a work of Deconstruction architecture.

用相機拍下老店舖，好作記錄。 *Trying to capture images for the old shops with my camera, so as to make a record.*

Queen's Road West to Central will be gone very soon. So, I will go take a walk there whenever it is possible, trying to capture on film those old tailor shops, herbal tea houses and dried goods stores …

　　上環的陳意齋賣的是小零食——涼果、話梅、嘉應子、蠔油豆和花生等，是十足十的香港製造，包裝也是十分香港，店內都是玻璃檯，店外的幾個大大的陳意齋招牌大字也是設計的典範。以前香港的店舖用字很講究，不像現在的電腦字，一點格局也沒有。有些老店會用黑底字，與白綠紅多種色的配合，不同的店有着不同的設計和用色方法，現在這些傳統在香港接近失傳。

Different kinds of snacks and munchies are sold at "Chan Yee Jai", the Hong Kong style snack shop in Sheung Wan: dried fruits, prunes, pears, dried beans and peanuts, all these are very original "made in Hong Kong" items, even the packaging is also very uniquely Hong Kong. There are glass cabinets all over the shop, and the signage of "Chen Yee Jai" in huge characters is also a classic design. In the old days, shops in Hong Kong were very particular on the wordings and style of their signage, not like the computer die-cut words nowadays. Some of the old shops would use gold characters on black, white, green or red in different combinations; with each having a different design and use of colours. These traditions are now vanishing in Hong Kong.

　　秋天在香港散步收穫特別多，可以較靜心看不同的事物。最佳的散步時間是早上六時，可看見不一樣的香港——特別的寧靜，空氣也特別清新，三兩報販在路旁摺疊報紙，乘客稀疏的電車在街上走，陽光漸漸明亮，風在吹，是很好的香港經驗。

One could experience more when strolling in Hong Kong during autumn, when one can watch various happenings with a peaceful mind. The best time for a stroll is 6 am, when one can see a different Hong Kong; it is particularly quiet with very brisk air. Two or three newspaper vendors stacking the day's paper at roadside, a tram with very few passengers passing by, the sun is getting brighter gradually, a gentle breeze… these are the wonderful "Hong Kong experience".

像這樣的老店，不知能保留多久。*Old shops like this are vanishing from Hong Kong.*

香港的都市空間十分多元化，有高大有中有小，有小街小巷也有大路，也有不同的高低，不像紐約和倫敦，都是平平的，只可以前看和向上看。香港的都市空間雖密集，但有層次感，每次從山頂散步到中環，再由中環散步到銅鑼灣，就有這種感覺。

The urban spaces of Hong Kong are diverse, some big and tall, some medium and some small in terms of scale, there are small alleys and backstreets as well as wide roads. There is also variance in levels, unlike New York City or London, which are rather flat, and can only be viewed from the front or above. Although the urban spaces in Hong Kong are concentrated, there is a sense of layering. I could feel this every time when I walk from the Peak to Central, and from Central to Causeway Bay.

秋天在香港散步，較在冷氣商場逛到處一樣的商店，有意思得多。

It is definitely more meaningful to take a stroll around Hong Kong in fall than to stay inside the air-conditioned shopping malls with identical chain stores.

早上6時沿著電車路散步，看見不一樣的香港，陽光漸漸明亮，風在吹，是很好的香港經驗。 *Strolling along the tramway at 6 o'clock in the morning, one could experience a different Hong Kong. With morning breaking and the breeze blowing, it is a very wonderful "Hong Kong experience".*

要與貝聿銘的中國銀行大廈做鄰居，又要維持鄰里和睦，確是一件不容易的事，嚴迅奇設計的花旗銀行大廈，用以柔制剛的方式柔化貝聿銘的刀鋒。 It is not an easy task to be neighbours with I.M. Pei's Bank of China Building and to maintain a harmonious relationship. The Citibank Tower designed by Rocco Yim has softened the sharp blade of Pei's building.

建築是城市記憶的標記
»Architecture is the Signifier of Urban Memory«

說起中環建築標記，即時想到貝聿銘的中國銀行大廈、科士打（Norman Foster）的匯豐銀行總部，又或是維多利亞式立法會大樓（舊高等法院）。無疑，這些風格強烈、性格鮮明的作品，都令過路人留下深刻印象。但中環建築還有另一種標記，就是本地建築師嚴迅奇（Rocco Yim）的作品。

When speaking of architectural landmarks in Central, one would immediately think of the Bank of China Building by I.M.Pei and the HSBC Headquarters by Norman Foster, or the Victorian-style Legislative Council Building (previously the High Court). Certainly these are fine works with strong style and clear identity that leave an impression on passers-by. However, there is still another kind of architectural landmark in Central, like the projects by local architect Rocco Yim.

街道旅程
A Journey through the Streets

不經不覺，嚴迅奇在過去十年已經為中環設計了五幢建築物：由花園道的花旗銀行大廈（前稱萬國寶通銀行大廈）開始，中環機場快線鐵路站、萬宜大廈、荷李活道房屋協會的荷李活華庭，到皇后大道

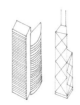

左 / 花旗銀行大廈：香港港島金鐘花園道3號
Left / The Citibank Tower: 3 Garden Road, Central, Hong Kong Island
右 / 中銀大廈：香港港島金鐘花園道1號
Right / The Bank of China Tower: 1 Garden Road, Central, Hong Kong Island

成報大廈面向雪廠街入口,保留了一個透明和通透的空間。 *The Ice House Street entry of Sing Pao Building has retained a transparent and open space.*

的成報大廈(註:成報大廈現名為中環皇后大道中8號)……,根據這些建築的地點,可以連結成一段段的街道旅程。

People might not be aware, but Rocco Yim has designed five buildings in Central during the last decade: the Citibank Tower on Garden Road, the Airport Express Hong Kong Station, Man Yee Building, Housing Society's Hollywood Terrace on Hollywood Road, the Sing Pao Tower (now named Queen's Road No. 8) on Queen's Road … an urban journey could be created through the linkage of these buildings.

　　從不同角度在建築物之間觀看這些作品,會發覺嚴迅奇在中環建立了一種標記:一種與中環街頭空間的對話。貝聿銘的中銀大廈與科士打的匯豐大廈是表現自我的風格表達,性格鮮明而強烈,是西方現代建築的典型作風。嚴則以互動的手法,與中銀大廈interact,與中環的街道interact,沒有鮮明的風格,沒有強烈的形態。像萬國寶通大廈,以柔制剛地把中銀的幾何三角刀鋒化解,深黑色的玻璃幕牆消化了中銀的反影,又大又高又明亮的大堂,是這座雙子大廈的精神所在,簡約而高雅。

Looking at these works from different angles among other buildings, one can find that Rocco Yim has established a landmark in Central: a dialogue with the streetscape. Pei's Bank of China Tower and Foster's HSBC Building are expressions of personal styles, with bold and strong characters, typical of Western modern architecture. Yim, in turn, has interacted in another way with the Bank of China Tower and the streets of Central, not with a distinctive style or a strong form. Take the Citibank Tower as an example: its gentle form softens the triangular blade of the Bank of China tower; its dark-coloured curtain wall absorbs the reflection of adjacent towers. Citibank Tower's atrium space is tall and bright, speaking well of the spirit of these twin towers – minimal and elegant.

　　沿着皇后大道中走，經過長江集團大廈、終審法院、匯豐銀行，最後走到在樹影之間的成報大廈。它坐落在三面單邊的位置，記得它以前是一幢啡色的圓形建築，坊間傳言指風水不太好，地下的店舖不停轉換租客，百貨公司及食店來來去去，於是業主決定拆卸重建。大廈的設計是圓加方，手法一貫地低調，心思都花在雪廠街入口的空間以及建築物的環保幕牆設計上，不是標奇立異，而是嘗試與四周的建築物和街道產生互動，融入中環的街道空間之中。

機鐵香港站簡潔、明亮的設計，令外國遊客對香港的第一個印象已感覺良好，國際城市的車站理應如此。 *The design of the Hong Kong Station is minimal and bright that gives a pleasant first impression to visitors, as how it should be for terminals of an international city.*

Walking along Queen's Road Central, passing by Cheung Kong Ltd. Building, the Court of Final Appeal, the HSBC Building, and finally arriving at the Sing Pao Building among tree shades, I remember there used to be a brown-coloured circular building on that site, standing there with three street-frontage, and it was said that the feng shui was not so good there: storefront tenants changed hands many times, department stores and restaurants came and went, eventually the owner decided to demolish and rebuild it. The new design is a composition of a circle within a square, a subtle signature of Rocco Yim. Thoughts were put on the entrance space on Ice House Street and the eco-curtain wall. It is not a spectacle, but an attempt to build an interactive relationship with the buildings and streets around, to blend into Central's streetscape.

　　中環是由不同闊度長度的街道所組成，經過百多年演變，發展成一種依山而起的街道網絡。建築的角色是配合街道網，建立一個統一而多元的街道空間。香港建築物設計的影響大都來自經濟利益壓力，歷史文化遺產觀念不受重視。中環百多年來的歷史建築大都被高樓大廈所取代，留下來的就只有一個街道網絡空間。建築師可以做的，就是利用這個街道網絡，來發展一些基本的創作語言及設計格式。嚴迅奇的中環作品就是在嘗試不同格式和語言，例如萬宜大廈部分的空間是典型的香港商業建築格式，唯一心思是花在巨型大廈與街道之間的關係之上。像皇后大道入口的處理，大廈分為上下兩部分，上半部的高樓貼近德輔道大街，令面向皇后大道的部分可以有更大更開揚的空間，為被高樓密封的皇后大道帶來陽光與空氣。萬宜大廈的電梯大堂空間也是一種簡潔的華麗，建築師在經濟壓力下，唯一可發揮的就只有電梯大堂的空間了！

Central is composed of roads of different lengths and widths. After a century's transformation, it is developed into a network of streets along the hill. The role of architecture is to work with this network of streets and build a unified yet diverse streetscape. The influence on architecture in Hong Kong came mostly from the pressure of economic interest; the concept of historical and cultural heritage is of no importance. What an architect can do is to utilise this network of roads to develop some basic design language and

機鐵站旁的國際金融中心商場會是中環另一個矚目的新作品。*The IFC Mall next to the airport express station is a new architecture in Central that would be an eye catcher.*

國際金融中心商場：香港港島銅鑼灣告士打道280號
The IFC Mall: 8 Finance Street, Hong Kong Island

style. Rocco Yim's projects in Central are attempts on different forms and architectural languages. For example, the spaces of Man Yee Building are characteristic of most typical commercial buildings in Hong Kong, but thoughts were put on the relationship between the giant tower and the streets. For example, Rocco Yim's treatment of the entrance on Queen's Road, it divides the building into two parts. The upper part is closer to Des Voeux Avenue, allowing the lower part facing Queen's Road to have a larger open space, bringing sunlight and air to this tower-packed road. The atrium space in Man Yee Building also possesses a simple kind of elegance; in this situation under strong economic pressures, the lift lobby became the only place where the architect could exercise his talent!

新的公共空間
New Public Spaces

二十世紀初的芝加哥高樓學派，其設計考慮不只是單純的經濟利

荷李活道附近的古董店。 *The antique shops near Hollywood Road.*

益和可租用面積，而是建築作為一種身份和藝術美學追求的象徵。「九七」之後香港樓市下調，可能造就了一種新的設計空間和美學身份。發展商競爭的重點將會由以前的空間大小轉移到設計美學。

Design considerations of the early 20th-century Chicago school were not solely on economic profit and lease-able spaces, but rather, architecture as a symbol of status and pursuit of aesthetics. After 1997, the property market in Hong Kong declined and that might have nurtured a new kind of design space and aesthetic identity. The competition between developers shifted from the size of space to design and aesthetic value.

由萬宜大廈沿皇后大道向前走五分鐘左右，便可看到嚴迅奇的住宅作品。住宅與商業大廈在香港以前都是混在一起的，近二十年政府引入西方分門別類的規劃準則後，商住混合慢慢被商還商、住還住的模式取代。荷李活華庭是依山坡而建的，一面是香港最具歷史價值的荷李活道，一面是皇后大道，三十多層高住宅被分成不同顏色的直條，與四周的舊大廈互相拼貼，單一巨大的體積化為一種建築物的多重組合。

Five minutes away from Man Yee Building along Queen's Road, there is the residential project by Yim. Residential and commercial buildings in Hong Kong used to mix together. Since about twenty years ago, the government introduced the western planning theory of separation of function, since then, mixed-use buildings were gradually replaced by single-use structures. Hollywood Terrace was built along a slope facing Hollywood Road, the road with the highest historical value in Hong Kong, with the other side facing Queen's Road. This tower of thirty-something stories is divided into vertical stripes of different colours; juxtaposing with the older buildings around, this singular large volume forms different collages with various compositions.

荷李活道是香港的古董店集中地，附近的摩羅廟街也是香港最古老的二手市場，三十多層的高樓與這些小街不成比例，旁邊四周與五棟樓房的對比實在非常勉強。這是香港城市空間的獨有現象，不需要考慮歷史，也不需要考慮Context，社區的Context，文化的

Context，想怎樣就怎樣，但一定要高要大，經濟利潤就是設計的指南針。

There is a concentration of antique shops on Hollywood Road, and Mosque Street nearby is the oldest antique marketplace. The thirty-storey Hollywood Terrace Tower is out-of-scale with nearby small streets; the contrast of these five towers with the surrounding is indeed far-fetched. This is a particular phenomenon in the urban space of Hong Kong, there is no consideration for history, the community or cultural context. Do whatever you like, but it has to be grand and tall, economical profit is the pointer for design.

　　房屋協會不是牟利的發展商，不是政府官僚架構，比較着重設計的質素，所以荷李活華庭有較多空間做設計實驗。住宅外表不是典型的單色外貌，也沒有所謂豪華的雲石大堂，單位是四四方方的平實，顏色的主調是灰灰藍藍，舊了也不會很難看。入口設計成為荷李活道與皇后大道的通道，演變出一種新的公共空間。

The Housing Society is a non-profit developer, and it is not a

荷里活華庭外牆是一條一條的顏色，嘗試將大型住宅融入小街之中。 *The vertical stripes of the façade of Holly Terrace are an attempt to mix the large-scale residential tower harmoniously into the surrounding small streets.*

government bureau, therefore they could concern more on the quality of design, allowing Hollywood Terrace to have more space for design experimentation. Its façade is not typically monochromic, and there is no so-called "luxurious" marble-lined lobby. The flats are fair and square, the colour tone is grey and blue that would not look bad with time. The entrance is designed to be a thoroughfare between Hollywood Road and Queen's Road, and has become a new type of public space.

大城市應有的氣質
The Temperament a Big City Should Have

　　至於中環機場快線鐵路站的設計是從功能出發，大堂空間是一種氣派，所有建築都應該有這種質素的空間。香港沒有像歐洲的大型火車站，其實大大的空間，就是大城市應有的氣質，中環機鐵站就變成了歐洲式的火車站，成為香港作為國際都會的空間標記。由機場到機鐵站，對香港的第一個印象一定是好的：明亮、快捷、簡潔、清楚。我知道嚴正在設計旁邊世貿中心的商場和酒店部分，開幕以後會成為中環最大的商業娛樂空間，究竟這是中環未來的新中心？還是另一個「大型地產項目」？這是近年香港最值得關注的建築事件。

As for the Airport Express Hong Kong Station in Central, the design originates from function. Its atrium possesses a type of style, space and quality that all architecture should have. There is no large train terminal in Hong Kong like those in Europe, although actually spaciousness is a temperament that a big city should possess, and Hong Kong Station has become a European-style train terminal, a spatial landmark of Hong Kong as a metropolitan. The journey from the airport to the Airport Express terminal in Central must give a good first impression of Hong Kong: bright, fast, simple and clear. I learnt that Yim is currently designing the adjacent shopping and hotel component of the World Trade Centre, it will become the prime commercial and entertainment space in Central after its opening. Whether this will become the future of Central, or another "large-scale real estate project" is what we should be concerned most among all architectural events these years.

大型樓盤的現代主義典範
»Models of Modernist Large-scale Housing Estates«

　　東薈城和東堤灣畔是近二十年香港大型私人屋苑中，最具建築空間感和完整設計理念的發展項目。負責建築設計的吳享洪是香港少數能夠成功地建立個人設計風格的建築師。位於大嶼山東涌的東薈城和東堤灣畔是他近年的代表作，他把香港典型的大型樓盤規劃設計概念，結合現代主義的設計語言和規劃原則。

The Citygate and Tung Chung Crescent are two large-scale private residential developments in Hong Kong that possess the most architectural sense of space and integrated design concept in the last 20 years. Anthony Ng Heung Hung, who was responsible for the design, is one of the few architects in Hong Kong who can establish a personal style successfully. These two projects on Lantau Island are his recent magnum opus; he has combined the planning concept of typical Hong Kong large-scale housing estate with the modernist design language and planning principle.

　　東堤灣畔的高層住宅樓宇不是典型的樓對樓格局，而是適當地安排在一個「合理」的位置，居住其中的人會擁有個人的景觀和空間。有意置業的朋友可考慮東堤灣畔，不但交通方便，住宅設計既實用也有空間——空氣流通，也看見山和水。香港很多處於山邊和水旁的樓宇，窗卻是小小的，方向也常常不對，光線暗淡，像一個密封的盒子。

The high-rise residential buildings of Tung Chung Crescent are not organised in a typical way in which towers are packed closely together facing each other. They are placed appropriately at a "reasonable" distance that residents would have their own personal view and space. For those who would like to buy a property can consider Tung Chung Crescent, it is not only well connected, but

讓住客擁有空間和景觀，是東堤灣畔所重視的。 *Tung Chung Crescent pays special attention to giving its residents a good sense of space and view.*

the design of the flats is also practical and spacious – with good air circulation and mountain and sea views. There are a lot of buildings in Hong Kong overlooking hills and the sea, however, they usually have tiny windows facing the wrong direction, and therefore are without much natural light like an enclosed box.

　　東薈城是連接地鐵與住宅之間的商場，簡單的設計予人空間感，細節的設計和營造也是香港異數。「God is in the details」，審視建築物的細節——柱子和地面如何連接、玻璃幕牆如何組合、窗台如何設計、雲石和地面的處理等等，會察覺到建築師的功力和設計心思。這些對細節的要求在東薈、東堤都可以找到。

The Citygate is a transit-mall that connects the MTR with associated housing estates. It has an austere space, and its construction details are also quite uncommon in Hong Kong. "God is in the details", so, when we observe architectural details closely, such as the column to floor connection, the composition of curtain wall, the making of windowsills, and the treatment of granite and flooring – one can see the strength and thoughts of the designer. These demands on details can be found in both Citygate and Tung Chung Crescent.

不作典型「樓對樓」的設計，東堤灣畔佈局高明。 *The buildings in Tung Chung Crescent are cleverly designed and organised not in a typical way in which towers are packed closely together facing each other.*

東薈城商場空間感甚強，可惜的是店舖不及商場設計那樣有特色。*The sense of space in Citygate Mall is very strong with an extraordinary ceiling height. Unfortunately, the shops there are mediocre chain stores without any character.*

　　東涌地鐵站的大堂找不到浮誇的雲石大堂，只見流線型的原汁原味石屎大柱、具層次感的燈光。再到東薈城商場，樓面比普通的高，所以空間感比較強，可惜的是所有店舖都是一般的連鎖店，沒有特色。我不明白發展商為何要執着這種沒有特色的商場，誰會傻得花時間老遠跑到東涌逛市中心常見的商場？

In the Tung Chung MTR Station one would not find flashy marble lobby, but just raw concrete columns and streamline forms, with lighting that has a sense of layering. Further into the Citygate Mall, it has a ceiling height higher than normal, so the sense of space is stronger than usual. Unfortunately all shops are mediocre chain stores without any character. I do not understand why developers insist on creating this sort of shopping malls with no distinctive identities, and who would be silly enough to spend time going to Tung Chung to find a mall just the same as those downtown.

淺水灣酒店
The Repulse Bay Residential Complex
淺水灣酒店是吳鴻亨較具爭議的作品。樓中間的四方形大洞無論如何
都是香港建築的重要個案。*The Repulse Bay Residential Complex is a
controversial work by Anthony Ng with a unique design. The empty square
in the middle of the building is definitely a significant and important case in
the history of architectural design in Hong Kong.*

　　如果是建築發燒友，又或者想得到多一點建築設計的「知識」，
參觀東薈和東堤是十分好的經驗。不少香港人花了一半以上的收入在
居住之上，卻未必得到合理的居住環境和生活質素——沒有風，沒有
陽光，沒有景觀，也沒有社區鄰里的空間——極像坐牢。

If you are an architecture enthusiast, or would want to know a little
more about architecture and design, it would be a great experience
to visit Citygate and Tung Chung Crescent. Most of us in Hong Kong
spend more than half of our income on our house, however, we do
not always get a reasonable place with reasonable environment and
living standard in return – it is always without air circulation, without
sunlight, without view, without community and neighborhood space
– just like being in jail.

山頂纜車站聖約翰大廈
Peak Tram Station, St. John's Building
吳鴻亨早期的建築作品，沒有花巧，簡簡單單的寫字樓和小小的車站，心思花在窗戶顏色和形態上。*The early architecture works of Anthony Ng Heung Hung are simple offices and small stations, not fancy at all. All thoughts were put on the designs and colours of doors and windows.*

東薈、東堤的客觀條件比市區好，有山有樹有風有水。和相似的愉景灣比較，東堤在佈局和設計上的水平明顯高得多。戶外公共空間的設計、植樹的規劃，都很配合環境，具有香港建築少有的氣派，屬於香港現代主義風格的代表作。

The conditions of Citygate and Tung Chung Crescent are relatively better than those in town centre, and there are hills and woods, wind and water. When compared to Discovery Bay that has similar conditions, Tung Chung Crescent is obviously better in terms of organisation and design. Its design of outdoor public space and landscape is in harmony with the environment, it has an aura that is rarely found in other architectures in Hong Kong. It should be regarded as a masterpiece of Hong Kong's modern architecture.

發展商能有這樣的勇氣讓建築師發揮，也是十分重要的，香港就是缺乏對建築和生活還有點要求的發展商。香港的建築師高手林立，缺乏的是發展空間。若果香港的公共房屋能由吳鴻亨設計，一定會比現在的更適合人類居住和生活。

It is also very important for developers to have the courage to allow architects to express and create on their own. What Hong Kong lacks are developers who have demands on the quality of life and architecture. There are all these talented architects in Hong Kong, but they lack space and opportunity to bring their talent and creativity into full play. If the public housing of Hong Kong can be designed by Anthony Ng Heung Hung, it would be more suitable for human habitation and living than what we have now.

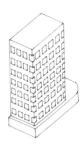

上頁 / 山頂纜車總站聖約翰大廈：香港港島金鐘花園道33號
Previous page / St. John's Building (Graden Road Terminus of the Peak Tram)：33 Garden Road, Hong Kong Island

物料的堅持
»The Choice of Materials«

香港可能是全球最大的意大利雲石買家，因為香港的建築設計對雲石已接近病態的沉溺。有雲石，就代表「豪」，代表「勁」，結果「豪宅」大堂與深圳ＸＸ休閒中心互相輝映。這種獨步全球的桑拿情意結是香港建築文化的精粹。

Hong Kong might be the world's biggest buyer of Italian marble because there is a pathological indulgence in marble in Hong Kong's architectural design. When there is marble, it means "extravagance", it means "awesome", and thus the lobbies of most luxury apartments look like sauna parlours in Shenzhen. This kind of sauna complex could be found only in Hong Kong, and is the very essence of the architecture culture of Hong Kong.

很多香港人對建築物的要求，停留在「物料平貴」的層面，所以意大利雲石與玻璃幕牆都成為香港建築物的必然要求，對建築空間的素質反而不太重視。建築空間與物料的運用存在着不可分離的關係，北京故宮的木結構木材料四合院佈局，元朗大夫第的磚石結構，香港新機場的鋼加玻璃結構，各自營造出不同的空間質素，光線、空間比例、質感都不一樣，身處其中會產生不一樣的心理反應。

The requirements on building materials for many Hong Kong people remain on the plain of whether the materials are cheap or expensive, and so Italian marble and glass curtain walls are the must have materials, and not much attention is paid to the quality of architectural spaces. The use of materials and architectural spaces are very closely related. Examples could be found in the wooden structure of the Forbidden City of Beijing, the brick structure of Tai Fu Tai Mansion in Yuen Long, and the steel and glass structure of Hong Kong's new airport. Each of these has its own unique quality and proportion of space, light and texture; and being in these structures would induce different psychological reactions.

公廁最重要的是空氣流通，建築師以結構來達到通風效果。 Air circulation is essential for public toilets. The architect here uses structure to achieve a good ventilation system.

香港人常誤以為用貴重的材料就保證獲取好的設計空間。其實空間的好壞取決於各種材料的配合，空間大小高低與人所產生的比例，及光線的強弱變化等。材料貴不一定是好。

Hong Kong people often mistake expensive materials as a guarantee for good space design. Actually, the quality of space design depends on the co-ordination of various materials with the space, such as the size and height of the space, the proportion, the variation of light. Expensive materials do not promise good space design.

鄭炳鴻，乙增至，勞建亮三人合組的ARCHI，正好示範了以材料運用為主體的建築設計風格，也是香港年青一代建築師之中，少數仍然維持以建築設計原則進行創作的組合。位於銅鑼灣維多利亞公園的公廁是他們示範的作品，這個作品也是透過公開設計比賽遴選產生。作品有幾個特點：首先打破了香港公廁是密不透風的形象；色調也不再是黑沉沉的，在白色的基礎上配上不同調子的黃綠藍，感覺很開揚；在結構上加強通風效果，造成一個不依靠冷氣的通風空間。

The architect trio "Archi", formed by Wallace Chang, Yuet Tsang Chi and Lo Kin Leung, is a very good demonstration of architectural design with materials as the main subject; and they are one of the very few groups which still maintain architectural design as their creative principle among the younger generation of Hong Kong architects. The public toilet in Victoria Park, Causeway Bay, is one of their works. This project is the winner of an open design competition, and has several special traits – it is the first to break away from the usual closed and suffocating design of toilet in Hong Kong; its colour tone is not dark and boring. It uses white as the base, and is sprinkled with different shades of yellow, green and blue, giving out a feeling of openness; with a strong ventilation system that does not rely on air-conditioning.

有意思的是整個建築雖然是現代主義風格，卻能營造出一種中國傳統建築的感覺。鄭、乙、勞都懂理論、設計及研究。好的設計都是由研究開始，好的設計師通常都很會做研究，愛觀察，被好奇心帶動。

維園的公廁有不少細節設計值得大家去發掘。*A lot of the design details in the public toilet of Victoria Park are worth our attention.*

What is interesting is that though the structure is entirely modernist in design, there is still a feeling of traditional Chinese architecture about it. Chang, Yuet and Lo are all well versed in theories, design and research. All good designs originate from researches, and good designers are usually exceptional in doing researches, with a passion for observation, and driven by curiosity.

　　香港大部分的業主都不太重視設計研究，主要是不想增加投資成本和延長建築時間。因此香港的建築空間大都是一式一樣，由政府公屋到半山豪宅到北角寫字樓，都喜歡重複相同的成功的方程式。在這情況下，建築師變得越來越不重要，好的設計一定建築費高昂的錯誤觀念也逐漸形成。

Most property owners in Hong Kong don't care too much about design research, mainly because they don't want to increase the construction costs or time. Thus, most architectural spaces in Hong Kong are more or less the same, may it be government public housing, luxury apartments in the Mid Levels or office buildings in North Point. They all like to follow the same successful formula. Under such circumstances, the role of architect becomes less and less important, and the misconception of good design equals to high construction costs becomes more and more widespread.

香港大學附近的摩星嶺青年旅舍，是鄭、乙、勞運用建築師智慧所創造的典範之作——建築費用低，建築空間質素高。結構是一般的石屎材料，心思都花在佈局及細節的設計上，絕對不是樣板港式建築。建築師充分顯示他們深刻理解建築的功能及與環境的關係。秋天在那裡宿營是一種靈性的經驗，風、樹木、天空……這是每個人都應該得到的經驗，這才是真正生活質素的指標。

Mount Davis Youth Hostel near the University of Hong Kong is also a project by Chang, Yuet and Lo. It is an exemplary work of design wisdom on the part of the architects – the construction costs are low and the quality of architectural spaces is high. Materials used are the usual like concrete, with all thoughts put on the design of the layout and details. It is definitely not the common Hong Kong style architecture, and its structure tells us how well the architects understand the function of the building and its relationship with the environment. Staying there in autumn is a spiritual experience, interacting with the wind, the trees and the sky … This is what everyone should experience, and this is what we call quality life.

在香港當建築師吃力不討好，尤其是有堅持的年青建築師，政府太官僚所以不太重視公共建築設計質素，地產發展商太功利所以無膽量嘗試不同的設計，而市民大眾在沒有選擇的情況下對建築空間的要求也不高。

Being an architect in Hong Kong is one hard job, especially so for young architects with ideals. Our government is too bureaucratic and does not care too much about the quality of design for public buildings; real estate developers concern themselves only with the interests of utility, and dare not try any different designs: while the requirements of the general public are not high since they do not have a lot of choices.

摩星嶺青年旅舍是馬會資助的產物，一幢建築的成敗往往是委託人與設計者合作成功與否的結果。享受如此高素質空間旅舍的，反而是國外來的旅客。 Mount Davis Youth Hostel is a project funded by the Hong Kong Jockey Club. The success or failure of an architectural work usually depends on the working relationship between the client/commissioner and the designer.

摩星嶺青年旅舍是用低成本建造出高素質的好例子。建築師用典型石屎物料來營造空間的佈局。*Mount Davis Youth Hostel is an exemplary work of high quality architecture with low construction costs. The architect uses typical concrete materials to create the layout of the space.*

其實建築本身不單是一門專業也是一門藝術，專業要發展得好，必須重視下一代的培育，以及研究工作。香港年青建築師面對最大的困局就是沒有一個健全的機制和文化，讓他們發揮和實踐其建築設計才能。建築是邊做邊學的學問，不可以紙上談兵，沒有機會實踐就沒有機會成熟。

Actually, architecture itself is not solely a profession, it is also an art. If we want this profession to be well developed, we have to put plenty of effort on nurturing the next generation and on research work. The biggest hindrance for young architects in Hong Kong is that we lack a sound system and culture for them to develop and realise their architectural designs. Architecture is a knowledge that one picks up as one practices it. It cannot be learned purely in the classroom, and there is no way to mature if there is no actual practice.

香港若希望出口其建築服務業，政府有責任提供更多機會讓年青建築師參與不同的公共建築設計項目，如公廁、學校、文化建築等等，除了能提升香港成為重視建築文化的城市，也能為香港旅遊業帶來更多「景點」，香港的建築師人才才不會被浪費。

If Hong Kong were to export its construction services, the government should take up the responsibility to provide more opportunities for our young architects to participate in various public architectural design projects, like public toilets, schools and cultural venues. In this way, it would be easier for Hong Kong to become a city that values architectural culture. At the same time, this would provide Hong Kong with more tourist attractions and help our tourist industry, and the talents in architecture would not be wasted.

石屎後遺症
»The Aftermath of Concrete«

石屎（即混凝土）是非常具彈性的建築材料，但相對於鋼鐵和木，它的壽命比較短（約一百年）。地產商為了求快，政府為了求快，大量使用石屎作為主要建築材料，並設計出一套倒模方法。倒模方法一般有兩種：一種是以木來造模，另一種是以鋼來造模。木是主流，因為較方便，但方便的後果是過去十多年來，香港已成為世界上入口木材最多的城市之一，這些木材大部分都不會循環再用，而是用作填海的垃圾。香港在過去十多年的泡沫繁榮期，浪費了數量多麼驚人的木材！

Concrete is a very flexible construction material although it has a shorter lifespan (about 100 years) in comparison with steel or wood. For the sake of speed as demanded by developers and the government, concrete has become the principal building material and a new casting method for concrete has been devised. There are generally two methods to cast concrete: one is casting with wood, the other with steel. The majority uses wood cast as it is more convenient, but the result of this convenience is that, in the last decade, Hong Kong became one of the cities with the highest timber import, and most of these timbers are not going to be reused but disposed for land reclamation. During the past ten years of Hong Kong's bubbling economy, timber has been wasted at an alarming rate!

「慢功出細貨」這句話有一定道理，所以過去十多年，政府和發展商那種瘋狂的建樓方法，將會為香港帶來很多後遺症。

The saying of "slow process gives fine product" must have its logic, and developers' and the government's method to build at a frantic rate in the last decade is going to bring many negative consequences to Hong Kong.

發展商的大型發展只顧利潤，空間是用盡了，卻換來一個個石屎監倉。 Developers care only about profits in their large-scale real estate projects. Spatial efficiency is maximised, but as a result we get blocks and blocks of concrete prison cells.

　　發展商的大型發展只顧利潤，空間是用盡了，但基本上是一座座貼了雲石片的監倉。香港身處亞熱帶，過去的建築設計也配合香港的天氣，所以露台成為一種非常具功能性的設計語言。一方面可以降低室內的氣溫，也可以使室內和室外空間產生聯繫。另一方面，露台也可以成為小型綠化空間或私人園林，平衡高層建築的監獄感覺。從環保角度和生活質素角度來看，露台是一種「必需品」。

In large-scale real estate projects that aim only for profits, certain spatial efficiency is maximised, however, the outcomes are essentially towers and towers of prison blocks with marble walls. Hong Kong is situated in a subtropical zone; the architectural designs in the past were in accord wtih Hong Kong's climate, with the balcony being very functional and a major part of the design language. On one hand, it can reduce indoor temperature and connect interior space with the outdoors; and it can also become a miniature green space or private garden, to balance the prison-like impression of towering architecture. From an environmental point of view as well as that of living quality, the balcony is a necessity.

　　但是由上世紀八十年代後期開始，露台只能是高官富人的專利品，露台已從香港的居住建築完全消失，消失的理由並不是設計上的因素，而是政府官員沒有重視人性、沒有建築設計的知識，訂立不重視人性的遊戲規則，鼓勵發展商興建一些不適合人類生活和社區發展的建築物。而最可憐的就是那些專業建築師，為了五斗米，違背專業知識的原則，設計出各種各樣不合乎設計邏輯和不適合人類健康生活的建築物。這些石屎建築，不單浪費大量材料，建成後也是一種依賴「冷氣」的建築物，每年浪費了大量電力，而由於興建速度過快，很多問題，如漏水、地陷等，將會在未來十年內陸續出現，將軍澳居屋就是一個例子。

However, since the late 80's, the balcony has become proprietary of the rich, and it has disappeared totally from Hong Kong's residential architecture. The reason of its disappearance is not a design decision, but the lack of consideration in humanities and architectural knowledge on the part of government officials. They had made the rules of game without considering the human factor, encouraging property developers to build projects that are not suitable for human living and community development. Architects of these projects are in a most miserable position. To make a living they would have to go against their professional principles and design all sorts of illogical and unhealthy buildings. With these concrete structures, excessive amount of materials is wasted in the construction process, and even after their completion they will become buildings that depend solely on air conditioning, wasting a lot of electricity each year. Because they were built too rapidly, many problems such as leakage or foundation settlement would appear gradually in the coming ten years, the government housing projects in Tseung Kwan O being a prime example.

石屎森林的陽光角度
»Sun-shading Angle in a Concrete Jungle«

　　過去香港的《建築物條例》有條文規定，樓宇設計興建時，必須顧及街道能夠獲得足夠的陽光照射，這對建築物的美感和環保作用均有幫助。不少舊區的民居仍保留着一級級一層層的梯級式建築形態，令陽光得以滲入街道。但自從這條文廢除後，香港街頭開始進入不見天日的日子。

In the past, there was a code in Hong Kong's building ordinance that regulated all building designs to ensure sufficient sunlight on the streets, contributing to both aesthetic as well as environmental considerations. There are still many residential buildings in the older neighbourhoods that have retained this stepped building architectural form with sunshine on the streets. However, since the day this building code was abandoned, the streets of Hong Kong started their days without sunlight.

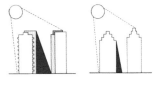

陽光角度的作用
The function of sun-shading angle
不同的建築物設計，會影響鄰近建築物和街頭獲得陽光照射的程度。右圖的建築物明顯可讓周圍得到更多陽光照射。*The design of a building will affect the neighbouring streets and buildings in their exposure to sunlight. It is obvious that the building in the photo on the right allows more sunlight around it.*

高樓建築往往將大街小巷完全包圍起來。*Very often, streets and alleys are completely surrounded by high-rise buildings.*

　　一個城市的建築設計風格與形態，是政府建築工程規劃機制與都市規劃方法的產物。香港的情況比較「極端」，在政府的高地價政策及着重建屋速度與數量的建築文化下，最能影響香港建築的，不是建築設計原則（Architectural design），而是政府的《建築物條例》（Building Ordinance）。

Architectural style and the form of a city is the product of its government's construction system and urban planning. The case of Hong Kong is rather extreme; with architectural culture under the high-land-price policy [1] of the government and emphasis on building speed and quantity, the dominant factor of Hong Kong's architecture is not architectural design but building ordinance.

　　《建築物條例》由屋宇署負責制訂和執行，地產商的目的是在最短的時間內興建最大的「可賣面積」，樓面的高度、窗戶的設計、空間的佈局……都僅僅達到條例的最低要求，所以自高地價政策推行之後，香港建築物的樓面越降越低。

The Building Ordinance is drawn up and carried out by the Building Department [2]. The objective of property developers is to build the largest "sell-able" space in the shortest time. The floor-to-ceiling height, the design of windows, and the organisation of spaces ... all reaching just the minimum code requirement. Therefore, ever since the implementation of the high land price policy, the floor-to-ceiling height of buildings in Hong Kong is getting lower and lower.

渣打銀行大廈：香港港島中環德輔道中4-4A號
The Standard Chartered Bank Building ; 4-4A Des Voeux Road Central, Hong Kong Island

1. High land price policy (高地價政策): a land use policy of the Hong Kong government that considers land sales to be the main revenue of the government.
2. Building Department (屋宇署): the government office that enforces the Building Ordinance and monitors safety and maintenance for new and existing buildings.

渣打銀行是香港高樓建築最重要的作品之一，也是最被「低估」的建築師 Remo Riva 最成熟的作品，大堂的空間特別精彩，像教堂的空間，充滿着歷史和時間質感。外表一級級的形態，是 Art-Deco 加上現代簡約的智慧。由置地廣場望向渣打銀行構成的「天空線」，是「中環十景」之一。The Standard Chartered Bank Building in Central is one of the most important works in Hong Kong high-rise architecture. It is also the most mature work of Remo Riva, one of the most "underestimated" architects. The space in the lobby is particularly amazing, like a space of a church, filled with a sense of time and history. The form of steps is a product of wisdom, with Art-Deco meets Minimalism. The skyline viewed from The Landmark towards the Standard Chartered Bank is one of the "Ten Wonders of Central".

不少舊區的民居仍保留着一級級一層層的建築形態。There are still many residential buildings in the older neighbourhoods that have retained the stepped building architectural form.

中環德輔道中
Des Voeux Road Central
中環是梯級式建築的集中地,德輔道中仍然保留着很多陽光角度型大廈,與遠處的中環中心形成非常強烈的對比。*There is a high concentration of stepped buildings in Central, and a lot of these structures with sun-shading angle are situated on Des Voeux Road. They form a sharp contrast to the skyscraper The Center, standing at a distance on Queen's Road Central.*

近年流行談環保,改革《建築物條例》本來是最有效推行「環保建築」的方法,但由於涉及太多地產商的利益及官僚架構的複雜權力關係,改革寸步難行。其實,只要條例規定樓底高一點、每戶必須興建露台、指定窗口必須裝置隔熱隔陽光的裝置(Sun shading device),就能夠達到節省能源及創造空間的功能。

In recent years, it is popular to talk about eco-design. Supposedly, a reform in the building codes would be most effective to bring about "environmentally-friendly architecture". However, since it involves too many complicated power struggles over the interests of developers and that of the bureaucrats, this reform is difficult to take place. In fact, should the codes only require the floor height to be a little bit higher, that each flat must have a balcony, or each opening must be equipped with sun shading device that can block sunlight and heat, the function of energy conservation and space creation could be achieved.

　　「陽光角度」的條文的存廢，代表香港高地價政策的分水嶺。戰後港英政府訂立此條文，規定每一條街道都能夠享受「足夠的陽光」照射，是保障香港高樓大廈發展的同時也要顧及環保和規劃城市景觀的需要。這個時期興建的樓宇，因而發展出梯級式的建築形態和設計。

The abolishment of the "sun-shading angle"–related codes created a watershed for land values in Hong Kong, resulting in a high-land-price policy. This building code was established by the post-war Hong Kong-British government, regulating that each street would have "enough sunshine", it was to ensure that at the same time of high-rise development, there would be considerations for environmental factors and urban landscape planning. For that reason, buildings constructed at that time should have a stepped form and design.

　　上世紀八十年代後期，港英政府為了推動高地價政策，並在各大地產商要求下，把這條最具環保價值的條文廢除。其後的香港高樓建築，就像萬里長城一樣，把大街小巷都包圍起來，形成了一條條「層峽」，是世界獨有的都市景觀———一幢樓高三四十層的大廈肩並肩排在一起，大廈之間的街道經常不見天日。這種場景在中半山堅道、羅便臣道、灣仔駱克道、謝斐道很常見。西方建築講求比例（Proportion）、大小對比（Scale）的規則在香港派不上用場。坐在雙層巴士的上層，在高樓森林裡穿梭，最能夠體會這種空間的力量，歐洲歌德式建築的室內超高空間在香港找到了對手。

In the late 80's, the Hong Kong-British government abandoned this eco-regulation for the sake of promoting the high land price policy under the demand from various large property developers. Thus, buildings in Hong Kong thereafter enclose all streets and alleys just like the Great Wall, creating folds of "street canyons" . It is an urban wonder that cannot be found elsewhere in this world – towers of thirty to forty-stories high lining up side by side, and one cannot see much sky from the streets among these towers. This sort of cityscape is quite common in Cannes Road, Robinson Road in the mid-levels, or in Lockhart Road and Jaffe Road in Wan Chai. The rules of western architecture regarding proportion or scale are not applied at all here in Hong Kong. One can experience strongly the power of this sort of space when riding on the top of a double-decker bus shuttling through this jungle of towers. The super-tall interior space of Gothic architecture in Europe might find a rival here in Hong Kong.

　　我們仍然可以在中環和一些舊區找到陽角度時期的建築物，梯級式的形態容許「空中花園」出現，建築物本身也營造了豐富的「天空線」（Skyline）。匯豐銀行總行面向皇后大道中的設計也因應陽光角度的要求分為兩級，旁邊的渣打銀行也追隨着陽光的角度一級級地分為四個層次。

We can still find some buildings that were built in the "sun-shading angle" era in Central or some older parts of town, the stepped form that allows the existence of "hanging gardens", and these buildings themselves also create a rich skyline. The Queen's Road Central-facing side of the HSBC Building has double-height levels in compliance to the sun-shading angle regulation; the adjacent Standard Chartered Bank Building also follows the sun angle regulation with its four-tiered design.

　　機場搬離九龍城後，九龍可能會出現更多高樓，這些高樓若果仍然在沒有陽光角度的指引下興建，香港的城市景觀和環境將會發生大災難！

After the international airport was moved from Kowloon City, there might be more high-rise towers popping up in Kowloon. If these towers were to be built without the guidance of sun shading angle, there would be a catastrophe on Hong Kong's urban landscape and the environment!

聖佐治大廈：香港港島雪廠街2號
St. George's Building : 2 Ice House St, Central, Hong Kong Island

聖佐治大廈是中環現代主義設計經典建築物之一，簡約而低調的坐落在文華酒店的旁邊，古銅色的玻璃幕牆特別講究細節。入口位於與文華酒店相隔的小街，電梯大堂是平實的高樓底空間，沒有浮誇的擬古典設計，外形按幾何角度分為兩個層次的比例，適當地配合街道的闊度。*St. George's Building is one of the classic buildings in Central with modernist design. It sits in low key and minimalism adjacent to the Mandarin Hotel; and special care was given to the meticulous details of the bronze glass curtain wall. Its main entrance is located on a small street opposite to the Mandarin Hotel. The lift lobby has a very high ceiling without any extravagant pseudo-classical design. The entire building is divided into two levels by sun-shading angle, and it is in perfect proportion to the width of the street.*

僑興大廈
Kiu Hing Mansion

坐落在英皇道14號的僑興大廈是香港梯級式民居建築的又一案例，其巨大的體積因應陽光角度的要求被切為一級級的立體派雕刻，面向天后廟道的層級就設計成不同大小的平台。由英皇道向維園方向望向僑興大廈的天空線，看見的除了有形態美，也能體會居民享受到陽光與空間的樂趣。 *Kiu Hing Mansion is another case of stepped residential building located on No.14 King's Road in Tin Hau. For the sake of maintaining a sun-shading angle, the building is cut into steps like a Cubist sculpture. The apartments on the side facing Tin Hau Temple Road are designed with terraces of different sizes. If you look at the building from King's Road in the direction of Victoria Park, the skyline is beautiful in shape, and you can also understand the pleasure of the residents enjoying the sun and a sense of space.*

沒有未來的香港建築師？
»Are Hong Kong Architects Without a Future?«

　　香港的冬天實在太短，通常二月份就開始潮濕。春天是十分可惡的季節，濕度高又時冷時熱，令人容易生病。幸而香港絕大部分的室內空間都有冷氣空調，問題是採用中央空調的大型商場長年冷氣開放，很多辦公室在冬天時仍然把溫度調得很低，浪費能源。

Winter in Hong Kong is way too short. Spring comes around in February and it starts to get humid, the high humidity and unstable temperature makes one sick easily and it is not the most pleasant weather in Hong Kong. Fortunately, almost all indoor spaces in Hong Kong are air-conditioned. However, it is a problem of energy waste, with shopping malls air-conditioned all year-round and a very low temperature is kept in most offices even during winter.

　　其實，衡量一座建築的價值，「美」不是唯一的標準，天氣、環保、心理、風土人情、歷史、社會、文化和政治也是重要的考慮因素和角度。建築師應要有社會責任感，有志以建築知識改善社會，令更多人可以生活在更美好的空間裡。然而，在香港要堅持當一個有責任感的建築師十分困難，原因是社會大部分人對建築的知識十分淺薄，大都慣於追求膚淺的快感。

In fact, appearance is not the only standard to judge the value of a building. Climate, environment, psychology, demography, history, society, culture and politics are also factors to be considered. An architect should have the social responsibility and a sense of mission to improve society with his/her architectural knowledge, letting more people to live in a better environment. However, it is very difficult to persist in being a responsible architect in Hong Kong. The reason being that most people in this society have only very limited knowledge on architecture; they are used to the pursuit of shallow pleasures.

　　建築是各樣藝術中要求最嚴格的，因為建築是人類生活的容器，不止是一件物件。好的建築師既要有美學修養，也要兼有工匠的技巧和工程師的頭腦。可惜現今的香港社會，最重視的是建築師的「管理」和「交際」能力，而不是設計能力。

Architecture has the strictest requirements of all arts; because architecture is the container for people to live in and not just an object. A good architect needs to be taught about aesthetics, as well as the skills of a craftsman, and has to possess the brain of an engineer. Unfortunately, in the current society of Hong Kong, "management" and "social/ networking" abilities of an architect are considered more important, and not his/her design skills.

　　建築師是香港眾多專業當中最可憐的，社會地位不及律師和醫生，賺錢不多，工作時間長，常常要受反智業主的氣，工作的滿足感不大，同行也不大團結。香港最大的建築師學會只注重短線的利益，鮮會批評行業裡不合理的運作。年輕建築師唯有轉行做室內設計，參與設計建築的機會少之又少。再過十年，會設計和堅持建築專業原則的香港建築師可能會後繼無人。

Being an architect is the most miserable among the many professions in Hong Kong. Their social status is not as high as that of the lawyers or doctors; they don't make a lot of money; their working hours are long; they always have to take ridiculous response from property owners; there is not much sense of accomplishment from work; and fellow architects are not so united either. The largest architect's association, the Hong Kong Institute of Architects, focuses merely on short-term profits, they would rarely criticise the abnormal operation in the industry. Young architects have no other way out that they have to move into the field of interior design, and there are less and less opportunities to participate in architectural projects. Ten years from now, there might not be any Hong Kong architect who can design and at the same time insist on professional ethics and principles of architecture.

建築師應要有社會責任感，有志以建築知識改善社會，令更多人可以生活在更美好的空間裡。遺憾香港這個短視的社會，並不重視建築師這個專業。
Architects should have a sense of social responsibility, aspiring to improve society with their architectural knowledge, and enabling more people to live in a better environment. Unfortunately, Hong Kong is a society which focuses merely on short-term profits, attaching no importance to the profession of the architect.

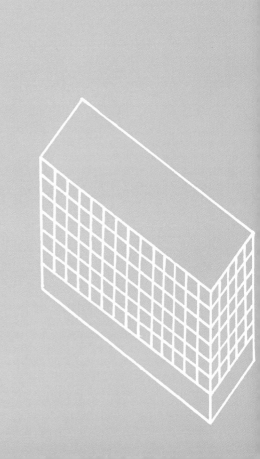

空間的性格與活力
The Character and Vigour of Public Spaces

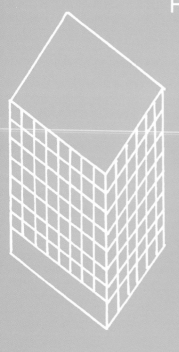
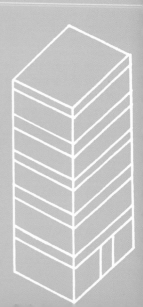

公園
»Parks«

　　在外地旅遊，公園往往是我的景點。如佛羅倫斯的文藝復興庭園 Boboli Garden、巴黎的盧森堡公園、紐約的中央公園、倫敦的St. James Park。

Parks are usually on my places-to-visit list while travelling abroad, such as, Boboli Garden, the elaborate Renaissance park in Florence, Luxembourg Park in Paris, Central Park in New York, or St. James' Park in London.

　　沒有人留意香港的公園，它們一直低調地存在於石屎高樓之間，卻是我們的集體記憶場所。

Not much attention is paid to the parks in Hong Kong. They lie low among concrete towers. However, they are places of our collective memories.

　　香港大大小小的公園約有二百多個，大部分都由政府的康樂及文化事務署負責管理，屬香港城市寶貴的公共空間。香港的公園沒有倫敦自然主義的片片草綠，亦沒有紐約中央公園的大森林，也沒有東京上野公園動物園博物館區的歷史文化氣質。

There are approximately two hundred parks, large and small, in Hong Kong. Most of them are managed by the Leisure and Cultural Services Department ; they are rare and precious public spaces of this city. Parks in Hong Kong do not have picturesque lawns as those in London, or forests as in Central Park, New York, nor do they have the aura of history and culture as Tokyo's Ueno Park with a zoo and museums.

　　我最喜歡的是中環前港督府對面的動植物公園，是典型香港殖民地時期的英式公園，重點是植物種類設計，邊走邊看着不同類型的大樹小植物，椰樹、榕樹、杉樹，有點像走進時光隧道，回到史前香港。

九龍樂富公園已是老公園,是街坊的活動場所。 *Lok Fu Park in Kowloon is an old park, a recreational venue for the neighbouring communities.*

公園是人的生活場所，並不是冷氣商場可以替代。香港的公園在都市森林的夾縫中生存，為我們開啟了一扇綠色窗戶。 *Parks are living space for humans, and they can never be replaced by air-conditioned shopping malls.*

The Botanical Garden in Central is my favourite park. Located across from the former Governor's Mansion (the Government House), it is a typical English-style park from Hong Kong's colonial period. It has a large collection of plants; and strolling in the garden, one can see different large trees and small plants along, quite like being in a time tunnel back to the pre-historic Hong Kong.

相隔一條馬路的香港公園，正好是一個反面對照，建築師非常刻意的要把公園設計出來，公園味道反而沒有了，像一個遊樂場，到處都是石屎地、建築物，沒有很多的綠；但裡面的茶具博物館就低調得多，而且是一種高調的低調，門前的草地也是中環最舒服的戶外空間。

The Hong Kong Park just across the street seems to give a negative contrast. The architect was consciously designing a park, yet the ambience of what a park should be is lost. It is more like a theme park, with concrete paving and structures everywhere and very little greens. However, the Flatstaff House Museum of Teaware in the park is rather understated, with lofty subtlety; its front lawn is also the most comfortable outdoor space in Central.

至於最出名應是維多利亞公園，翻新工程也接近完成，新設計把以前那種被圍堵的感覺打破，圍欄低了，行人路好像闊了，新維園將會是香港重要的標記和公共空間。集會、「六四」燭光聚會、踢足球、打籃球，各式各樣的運動和活動、早上晨運耍太極、星期天舉辦《城市論壇》（按：討論時事的現場直播電視節目）……維園是香港多元社會的寫照。

The most well known park in Hong Kong is Victoria Park in Causeway Bay. After its recent renovation, the new design breaks through from the previous enclosed feeling: the fences were lowered and the sidewalk seems to have been widened. The new Victoria Park is going to become Hong Kong's important landmark and public space, with public congregations, candlelight vigils for June 4th, football or basketball games, all sorts of sports and activities, tai-chi in the morning, City Forum on Sundays … Victoria Park is a portrait of Hong Kong as a diverse society.

從中環動植物公園望過去，香港的大都會感覺十分強烈。 *Overlooking the city from the Zoological and Botanical Gardens in Central, we could feel that Hong Kong has a very strong sense of a metropolis.*

　　香港的老公園其實不少，但大都在這幾年被改得面目全非，尖沙咀覺士道公園就是典型例子，以前簡簡單單的鞦韆、沙地，被一些五顏六色的新遊樂設備取代。附近是九龍半島最大的公園——九龍公園，由於昔日是軍營，改建之前十足一個探險公園，有舊營房與防空洞，山坡與草地；改建後，照明設施改善了，活動空間規格化，喜歡大自然風格的，會覺得太人工化，失去了以前的神秘感、自然格調和古舊的歷史感。

There are actually quite a few old parks in Hong Kong, although almost all of them have changed radically in recent years. A typical case is the park in Cox's Road in Jordan-Tsim Sha Tsui. There used to be simple old-fashioned swings with a sand ground, but they are now replaced by some colourful plastic recreation equipment. Nearby is the largest park in the Kowloon Peninsula – the Kowloon Park. It used to be a military camp in the past; before renovation it was like an adventure park with barracks and bomb shelters, slopes and lawns. After the renovation, illuminating facility is improved and activity spaces are formalised. For those who prefer parks of a natural style would think it has become too artificial and has lost

九龍城寨公園變了江南庭園，完全與城寨歷史割裂。 *The Kowloon Walled City Park is a traditional Chinese-garden park, without any traces of the history of the former ghetto of Kowloon Walled City.*

九龍公園經重新設計之後，失去了以前的自然風格，變成另一個石屎式的主題公園。 *After its redesign, Kowloon Park has lost its natural touch, and has become another theme park in concrete.*

its sense of mystery, and the natural and historical atmosphere of the past.

九龍仔公園和摩士公園都是老公園的代表，九龍仔公園以前最出名就是那個小型高爾夫球場，打的不是甚麼草地洞，而是一個個主題石屎地「球場」，有中式和西式的。兩個公園都有泳池，九龍仔的歷史比較長，有點像維園泳池風格，特別的是有一個形狀不規則的泳池，往日鄰近機場，附近高樓大廈不多，因此住在政府屋邨的街坊在中秋節時總會到摩士比拼燈籠。這種街坊氣氛已淡化了，可能是因為政府規管太多，甚麼都不准，節日的情懷也冷卻了。

The Kowloon Tsai Park and Morse Park are the representatives of older parks. Previously, the Kowloon Tsai Park was known for its mini-golf course, it was not a golf course on the lawn, but one in concrete in Chinese-and-western style. Both parks have swimming pools; the one in Kowloon Tsai Park has a longer history, similar to that of Victoria Park, its feature is an organic-shape pool. When the airport was still nearby, there were not many tall buildings, and thus this park seemed more spacious. In Morse Park, there is an open-air theatre, with many public housing estates nearby, the neighbours would gather for informal "lantern contest" in mid-autumn festival. However, this sort of neighborhood atmosphere has faded, perhaps due to the government over regulation and prohibition for everything, so along it goes the festival mood.

以前的九龍城寨，則變了傳統的中式庭園公園，僅保留了城寨中心的那座祠堂。外國朋友只能在相片和影片找到昔日城寨的風味。香港政府近年建設的公園總喜歡標榜所謂主題式概念，像荷李活道公園和寨城公園等等，藉詞以中國文化為設計概念，公園已不再是市民交流活動的場所，淪為演繹中國偽園林藝術的怪地方。

The previous ghetto of Kowloon Walled City has now become a traditional Chinese-garden park, only remaining is the shrine at the centre. Nowadays, visitors can only find the impression of the old ghetto in photos and films. Public parks constructed by the government in recent years tend to emphasise on concepts which are theme park oriented, such as the park on Hollywood Road or

金鐘香港公園 *Hong Kong Park in Admiralty*

新維園行人道 *The pedestrian walkway of the new Victoria Park*

the Kowloon Walled City Park, They claim to have used Chinese culture as the design concept, yet these parks are no longer leisure places for social activities and exchanges for local people, but have become some bizarre places of fake Chinese gardens and landscape.

大埔海傍公園則比較能發揮公園的功能，其設計有點蘇聯上世紀二十年代建構主義（Constructivism）的味道，佈局的手法、空間與建築物的佈置、與海邊的關係，都有板有眼，裡面是建構主義的複製品，其空間比例和細節設計是少有的用心。

The Waterfront Park of Tai Po has performed the function of a park to a fuller extent. The design has a touch of Russian Constructivism of the 1920's; its organisation, spatial relationship with placement of structures, and the relationship to the waterfront are all nicely executed. There are replicas of constructivism structures in the

以上世紀二十年代蘇聯建構主義風格作設計的大埔海傍公園，竟呈現了另類色彩；公園內的回歸紀念塔，可有微言大義？ *The Tai Po Waterfront Park has a taste of Russian Constructivism of the 1920's in its design, giving it some alternative flair. Is the Tai Po Lookout Tower in the Park (established for the commemoration of the transfer of sovereignty of Hong Kong in 1997) bearing some implication or profound messages?*

park, with outstanding and well-thought-out spatial proportions and design details.

尖沙咀的海濱公園本應有很大的潛質，由尖東走向文化中心的那一段路是香港十景之一，可惜規劃不太好，空間狹窄，變成一條走廊。理想的方案是把尖東海旁的高速公路移到地底，路面改建為廣場，闢為行人專用區，多種些大樹，多些露天茶座或大排檔。

The Harbour Side Park of Tsim Sha Tsui was supposed to have great potentials, the walk from TST East to the Cultural Centre is one of the top 10 attractions in Hong Kong. Unfortunately it is poorly planned, spaces being very narrow and tight that they have become a corridor. An ideal proposal would be to move the harbour side highway underground, turning the road surface into a pedestrian plaza, and to plant more trees and have some open-air cafes or "dai pai dong" (Chinese street food stalls) along.

油麻地政府合署後面的公園位處廟街附近，早上有老人家在下象棋、談天，老式的香港生活每天在上演。古廟、老樹，見證着油麻地區的變化。公園是市集，也是求神問卜、市民強身健體的場所。冷氣商場的出現，不經不覺已取代了某些的「公園」功能，但公園始終是公園，樹、天空、草地、空氣是冷氣廣場不能提供的。

Behind the Yau Ma Tei civil complex, there is a park nearby Temple Street. There are elders playing chess or chatting in the morning; the old Hong Kong lifestyle is on display here every day. The aged temple and old trees have witnessed the transformation of the Yau Ma Tei district. The park is also a market; as well as the place for fortune telling and exercising. With the birth of air-conditioned shopping malls, some functions of the park were taken up by the malls without being noticed. However, a park is a park. The trees, the sky, the lawn and the air are something that an air-conditioned plaza can never provide.

文字建築
»Architecture with Texts«

混合用途建築是香港獨特的奇景，衍生出來的建築物外牆被文字包圍着，反映香港平民百姓的民間智慧和設計風格。

Mixed-use architecture is a unique wonder in Hong Kong. The facades of these mixed-use structures are covered by signs with various typographies, which reflect folk wisdom and typical local styles of design.

一九七零年代以前，香港土地用途的規劃比較隨意，容商住混合用途的建築物出現。之後香港政府慢慢引入西方現代規劃的觀念，用畫格仔的模式把土地用途具體地規管，商業就是商業，住宅就是住宅，學校就是學校，分得清清楚楚。

Prior to the 1970s, planning of land use in Hong Kong was rather arbitrary, allowing buildings to have mixed-function of residential and commercial purposes. Later, the government of Hong Kong introduced concepts of western modern planning, governing land use with a checkerboard method – designating commercial zones for commercial use, residential areas for residential purpose, school areas for educational institutes, with everything in clear divisions.

現在「保存」下來的商住混合建築，從城市規劃、社會發展、經濟發展的角度，以至從建築設計的美學風格分析，都極具啟發性。商住混合是中小型企業的基地，是傳統手工藝（如洋服、打金）的最佳工作空間，尖沙嘴的美麗都大廈、重慶大廈就是很好的例子。

The mixed-use structures that are "preserved" till today are very inspirational in terms of urban planning, social and economic development, as far as architectural design and aesthetic analysis are concerned. These mixtures of residential-commercial uses are the bases of operation for small and medium enterprises; they are ideal ateliers for craftsmen with traditional trades (such as tailors

佐敦道勁力健美中心是香港的老牌健身室，外牆的紅字白底十分搶眼。晚上光管全開，沒有冷氣，所有窗戶打開，裡面的健身人在強烈的白光管下做健身活動，是佐敦道奇景之一，也是混合用途建築的一種獨有風格。小時候到裕華國貨買買零食路過，總是好奇地想着那些肌肉人在做甚麼。 *There is a very old fitness centre in Jordan, and its sign with the bright red figure and characters facing the crossroads is extremely eye-catching. During the evening, with no air-conditioning, its windows are all wide open and the room is brightly lit. One can see people working out inside under the glaring light of the fluorescent tubes – this is quite a sight and a wonder of the Jordan district, this also reflects the unique style of mixed-use architecture. When I was a kid, I always passed by this spot on my way to Yue Hwa Chinese Products across the road to buy myself some snacks, and I always wondered what those muscle men were doing up there.*

and goldsmiths). Mirador Mansion and Chungking Mansion in Tsim Sha Tsui are good examples.

自由發揮生活工作場所
The Live-work Place of Free Expression

灣仔、銅鑼灣、旺角、筲箕灣、油尖旺、深水埗等香港舊區是混合用途建築的集中地，這些建築物裡，有醫務所、道觀、基督教教堂、學習中國功夫的教室、中國傳統書畫的畫室學院、書店、洋服工場、寫字樓、宗親會聯誼會工會、區議員辦事處、一樓一鳳、健身室、幼稚園等等民間自由發揮的生活工作場所。

Wanchai, Causeway Bay, North Point, Shau Kei Wan, Yau Ma Tei, Tsim Sha Tsui, Mongkok, and Sham Shui Po are the old districts in Hong Kong with high concentration of mixed-use buildings. Inside these buildings there are clinics, Taoist shrines, Christian houses of prayer, schools for learning Chinese kung-fu, studios giving lessons for traditional Chinese painting and calligraphy, bookshops, tailor shops, offices, clubs and clubhouses for families, societies and labour union, offices of council members, brothels and apartments where individual sex workers provide services, gyms, kindergartens, etc... all kinds of spaces created randomly by folks of different trades and beliefs.

這種狀況與現香港政府那種「原教旨控制式」的西方規劃概念格格不入，政府也沒有好好研究這種混合用途建築的好處，在規劃時引入一些混合概念，改良目前混合用途在管理上的弱點。而市區重建局（前身為土地發展公司）在重建時，只會把原有舊區的混合用途消滅，引進一些所謂「高級」、「現代」的太空館式大型商場建築和一式一樣的住宅大樓。

This situation does not fit in with the government's "fundamentalist control" planning point of view, but the government did not take the chance to study the advantages of this mixed-use concept and incorporate it into their planning so as to improve and get rid of the current weaknesses in managing the development of mixed-use

建築物內各商舖的用途，從外牆文字已可反映出來。（拍攝於翻新工程前）
One can tell the purpose and use of each unit in the building by the look and the text of the signage on the façade. (the photo was taken before renovation)

旺角彌敦道新興大廈是混合用途工作的有趣個案，有桑拿、夜總會、卡拉OK、一樓一鳳等以色情娛樂為主題的 Theme Park Building（主題公園大廈），以前港大建築系曾經有人建議以新興大廈作個案分析，並以此發展新一代的香港色情娛樂主題的混合用途建築，聽說後來被否決了。Sun Hing Building on Nathan Road in Mongkok is a very interesting case of mixed-use structure. There, you have saunas, nightclubs, karaoke bars, brothels and apartments where individual sex workers provide services. It is like a theme park building with all sorts of venues for adult entertainment. Some while ago, a student in the Department of Architecture in HKU proposed using Sun Hing Building as a case study to develop a model of the new generation mixed-use architecture for adult entertainment venues. Later I heard that the proposal was rejected.

architecture. When the Urban Renewal Authority (previously Land Development Corporation) works on a rebuild project, they would only destroy the existing mixed-use structures and bring in some so-called "high-end" or "modern" giant shopping malls which look like a space museum and residential towers which look more or less the same.

混合用途建築之所以是香港風格的奇景，是因為建築物與文學產生的化學作用，建築物的外牆被文字包圍着，功能上文字成為空間用途的代號，讓街上的途人能夠閱讀和知道個別單位的功能和用途。這些文字的組合、字款的設計，為平平無奇的石屎建築帶來了一種充滿動感和活力的景象。

Design considerations of the early 20th-century Chicago school were not solely on economic profit and lease-able spaces, but rather, architecture as a symbol of status and pursuit of aesthetics. After 1997, the property market in Hong Kong declined and that might have nurtured a new kind of design space and aesthetic identity. The competition between developers shifted from the size of space to design and aesthetic value.

與西方成強型對比
Strong Contrast with the West

外牆文字招牌的設計，十分多元，顏色配搭有紅加白、有黑加金，字體有毛筆書法字、有仿宋克體，製造方法有凸字、有凹字，有手寫、有木刻、雲石麻石石雕、有霓虹光管。混合用途建築不是業主和建築師尋求單一美學風格的場所，而是容許每家每戶各自發揮表達其個性的平台，也是不同類型工匠發揮和比練功力的場所。

The design of exterior signage is diverse and pluralistic. There are the red/white, black/gold colour combinations; the fonts could be calligraphy, serif or sans serif; they are made in relief or etching; the form varies from hand writing, wood craving, granites/ travertine to neon tubes. In mixed-use architecture, it is not the proprietor or architect seeking for a particular aesthetic style, but a platform allowing expression by each individual household; it is also the arena for craftsmen to compete their skills.

　　這種多元和雜亂的美學風格與西方追求「統一設計」語言形成強烈對比，反映了香港混合多元社會的本質與西方界線分明的多元概念是不同的。

This diverse and chaotic aesthetics is in strong contrast to the "unified design" as advocated by the west. It exhibits the mixed and diverse nature of the society of Hong Kong that is fundamentally different from the clear and simple western concept.

　　其實兩個市政局時期發展的市政綜合用途大廈是很好的概念，但在設計形式上涉及太多官僚程序，反而太少設計研究和鼓勵不同形式的設計，導致市民大眾對混合用途的概念存有誤解。無論如何，混合用途是香港風格不可或缺的一種建築模式。

As a matter of fact, the concept of mixed-use municipal buildings from the time of the former Urban Council was a very fine one. However, in terms of design, there were too many bureaucratic procedures, and too little design research and encouragement for different designs, thus causing a misunderstanding in the concept of mixed-use for the public. Anyhow, mixed-use architecture is one indispensable model of Hong Kong style.

霓虹世界的盡頭
»At the End of the Neon World«

香港是全世界最光亮的城市，入黑以後，由偏遠的小村落到旺角到中環，街上都是光亮的。可能因為電費太便宜，或是治安理由，香港的夜色特別明亮，高樓大廈像燈飾一樣發光發亮，把天空照得像白天一樣。遠望像燈飾，走進大街大巷，則是另一種光景——鬧市的招牌立體地介入街頭的空間。

Hong Kong is the most illuminated city in the world. From distant villages to Mongkok to Central, the streets are all bright even after dark. Perhaps electricity is too cheap, or for safety reasons, the nights in Hong Kong are particularly bright. High-rise towers are lit up like Christmas trees brightening the night sky, making it look like daytime. Viewing from a distance, it looks like a city with Christmas lights, and when you walk in the streets it turns into another picture – signage and billboards are hanging three-dimensionally above the streets.

大大小小的商店招牌在街頭凌空掛着，最突出的是霓虹招牌。由於這裡不是地震區，所以其他城市不可能發生的事，很多都可以在香港發生。試在任何一個夜晚，坐在雙層巴士的上層，由尖沙咀出發，沿着彌敦道一直走，或者在旺角西洋菜街、女人街（通菜街）的行人專用區漫步，又或選擇在秋天的晚上開坐在電車的上層，由西環出發，沿着德輔道、軒尼詩道、英皇道緩緩走着，都可以欣賞到大大小小的霓虹光管招牌層層疊疊，構成香港最壯觀的城市景象之一。

Shop signs, large and small, are suspending in mid-air, and the ones in neon lights are most outstanding. Since Hong Kong is not an earthquake zone, many things can happen here that are quite impossible elsewhere. Taking a bus-ride on the top deck at any night, starting from Tsim Sha Tsui along Nathan Road, or taking a stroll in the pedestrian zones of Sai Yeung Choi Street and Ladies' Street (Tong Choi Street), or picking a cool autumn night to ride on

來佬餐館
LOYAL DINING

霓虹招牌的風格充分反映了香港是個複雜而矛盾的城市。 *The unique style of Hong Kong's neon signs fully reflects the complicated and contradictory nature of our city.*

Neon Signs *Neon Signs*

霓虹光管於1910年由法國物理學家 Georges Claude（1870-1960）發明，透過高壓電流與氖 (neon) 氣體產生化學作用，產生一種深紅色光線。以此為基礎，透過不同種類的氣體與高壓電的實驗，發展出後來五光十色的霓虹招牌。*In 1910, French physicist Georges Claude (1870-1960) invented the first neon lamp, and soon neon lighting quickly became a popular fixture in outdoor advertising. Glass tubes are filled with neon gas, which produces a red glow when charged with high voltage electric current. When other gases are used, they produce different frequencies of radiation and therefore different colours.*

古典與Kitsch
Classical and Kitsch

鏞記是香港的經典中菜館，對面的翠華是近年中下價食店的後起之秀，兩個霓虹招牌放在一起，對照出他們的性格：鏞記的招牌是那種經典式的四平八穩，字體工整，格式整齊簡潔；翠華的動感巨型霓虹光管屬市井的Kitsch（庸俗）那類，五顏六色，令人眼花繚亂，倒搶了鏞記不少風頭。*Yung Kee in Central is a classic Chinese restaurant, and situated across the street is Tsui Wah, the rising star restaurant of these last years. When seen side by side to each other, the neon signs of these two restaurants bring out the great contrast in their characters: Yung Kee's signage is the very neat and traditional kind with strong and proper typography; while the huge neon sign of Tsui Wah is flashy and kitsch, dazzling with all sorts of colours, and stealing the thunder of Yung Kee.*

鏞記酒家：香港港島中環威靈頓街32-40號
Yung Kee Restaurant: 32-40 Wellington Street, Central, Hong Kong Island
翠華餐廳：香港港島中環威靈頓街15-19號
Tsui Wah Restaurant: 15-19 Wellington Street, Central, Hong Kong Island

大金龍 *The Golden Dragon*
香港的老麻將館保留了很多香港的老式設計風格。位於灣仔舊區的大金龍是
其中的表表者，霓虹招牌仍然用香港老式的龍鳳設計概念，手工十分精細。
The old mah-jong parlours in Hong Kong retain a lot of traditional Hong
Kong style designs, and "The Golden Dragon" located in the old district of
Wanchai is one good example. Its neon sign is old-fashioned and classical,
with very well wrought and intricate dragon and phoenix design.

the top deck of a tram going slowly from the Western district along
Des Voeux Road, Hennessy Road and King's Road, one can view
the layering of neon light signage of various scales that creates one
of the most magnificent urban sceneries of Hong Kong.

　　香港風格是一種充滿矛盾和複雜的設計語言，霓虹招牌林立營造
出不統一的都市空間。在機場仍然設在市中心的日子，城裡的霓虹光
管雖然都是靜態的裝置，不如東京和拉斯維加斯的圖案跳躍閃動，但
也有異於東京、拉斯維加斯的招牌那樣平面地「貼」在建築物上，而
是立體地介入了街道空間。

"Hong Kong Style" is a complicated design language full of
contradictions; the abundance of neon signs makes up a non-
uniform cityscape. In the old days when the airport was still at the
city centre, neon signage in town was static installations. Although
they were not blinking patterns as those in Tokyo or Las Vegas, they
differed from those in these two cities where signs are "pasted" flat
on buildings. The neon signage in Hong Kong intersects into the
space of the streets three-dimensionally.

解放前的上海也是霓虹招牌的天堂，解放後這種資本主義的符號
消失了一段日子，改革開放以後又逐漸在中國各大城市出現，只是解
放前的那種細緻工藝已經失傳。霓虹光管是一種工藝，舊當舖的招牌
是好例子：簡單的曲線構圖、紅色的光線，看似教堂的十字架標記，
令人過目難忘。

Shanghai, before the 1945 liberation, was also a heaven of neon
signs. These capitalistic symbols disappeared for a while after
the liberation. Since the reformation and open-door policy of
China, they reappeared in various large cities gradually; only that
intricate craftsmanship was lost since. Neon signage is a craft. For
example, we can see from the signage of old pawn shops: a simple
composition of curves in red lights, this symbol that looked like a
crucifix left an unforgettable impression.

機場遷離市區後，香港的霓虹招牌就「動起來」，翠華茶餐廳和
扒王之王等連鎖式食店、大大小小的夜總會娛樂場所都爭相引入動畫
式的霓虹光管。最巨大的和最奇特的，當數中環中心由電腦燈光設計
的變色「糖果」，有一次我從山頂望下去，見它在慢慢變色，從黃到
紅、紅到綠、綠到藍、藍到白……像會與人溝通的生物。身邊的朋友
說它像一條舊式三色冰條，很可愛。

Since the airport has been moved from the city centre, neon signage
in Hong Kong has been "on the move", food chain stores such as
Tsui Wah and Steak Expert; night clubs and entertainment venues,
all make haste to introduce animated neon lights into their signage.
The largest and most eye-catching would be the computer-
controlled changing lights of The Centre, located on Queen's Road
Central. Once I was looking down from the Peak, and seeing its
colour changing gradually from yellow to red, red to green, green
to blue, blue to white… just as a living thing communicating with
humans. My friend next to me said it looked adorable and was like
the tri-colour popsicle from the old days.

光是空間之母，是最神聖的；歌德式（Gothic）建築物就是光線
的容器。電燈發明以後，光不單是空間的材料，也是一種變化多端的
媒體。香港處理光有自己的一套，不注重光與空間的互動，而是強

調光的照明功能和影像效果，並以它來構成一種符號。可能由於是這樣，晚上在山頂看香港與早上看的感覺很不一樣——早上是看死物，晚上就能看到由不同光點組成的流動影像，像生物一樣。

Light is the mother of space - the most sacred; and Gothic structures are the containers of light. Since the invention of electric light, light is no longer just a spatial rendering material, but also a medium of many changes and possibilities. Hong Kong has a unique way of treating light that does not emphasise on the interactions between light and space, but stresses on the illuminating function and visual effects, and furthermore, constructing it into signifiers. Perhaps it is for this reason that the view of Hong Kong from the peak during the day is very different from that of the night. During the day, it looks dormant; but at night, one can see a moving image composed of different spots of light, just like a living creature.

中區與半山的行人電梯，把過客與兩旁的居民，活生生的扯在一起，人在途中如觀看萬花筒。 The lives of the pedestrians and residents on both sides of the escalator walkway between Central and the Mid Levels are pulled together in time and space by the escalator. Walking along it, one sees images after images like looking into a kaleidoscope.

天橋天地
»A Domain of Flyovers«

香港是使用天橋和行人天橋最有特色的地方。
In Hong Kong, flyovers and footbridges are most peculiarly and interestingly used.

先不談美學問題，香港的天橋有很強的功能性和實用性，像中環至半山的行人電梯天橋，灣仔告士打道的行人天橋或行車的東區走廊。
Putting aside the issue of aesthetics, we can see that the flyovers in Hong Kong are highly functional and practical, like the Central-Mid-Levels escalator walkway, the footbridges of Gloucester Road or the Eastern Corridor Expressway.

天橋也為香港營造很多非常具戲劇性的都市空間，像從半山薄扶林道連接西環山道的天橋，行車的橋面就像日本卡通「鐵甲萬能俠」裡的出擊跑道，橋底形成高而巨大的歌德式空間。夏天盂蘭節時橋底搭建起一座竹棚劇場，看似解構主義建築作品。
The various flyovers and bridges in Hong Kong also help create a lot of dramatic urban spaces, such as that at the overcrossing of the flyover connecting Pokfulam Road in the Mid-Levels and Hill Road in the Western District. The overpass with running cars looks like the runway for piloted robots in the Japanese anime Mazinger Z, while the tall and huge space under the bridge looks very Gothic; and during the Hungry Ghost Festival in summer, the temporarily erected bamboo theatre under the bridge seems like an architectural work of Deconstructivism.

由西區海底隧道至長青隧道一段路，穿插在旺角和深水埗新新舊舊的高樓大廈之間，像在半空裡盪漾，看見的城市景觀和地面上看的完全不同，真是香港的十大奇景之一；舊機場天橋也有相類的電影感效果。

西環山道天橋是相當獨特，不單坡度陡峭，彎急路面窄，橋底高聳更差不多是全港天橋之冠，這是香港地狹民居稠密的衍生產物。*The flyover at Hill Road in Western District is quite unique. Its slope is steep, and its curves are sharp. It stands tall, towering, and is among the highest flyovers in Hong Kong. This is the product of a small city with high urban density.*

中區的行人天橋，它是世界上少見的行人天橋系統，差不多將這個商業心臟內的主要建築物連在一起，貢獻可不少。灣仔柯布連道天橋的人流，部分就是由這些分支疏導和匯集起來的。*The Central Elevated Walkway is one of the very few extensive walkway network systems in the world. It plays a very important role in commuting in Central because it links up almost all the major buildings of this commercial area, making great contribution to the district. These branches are converging and diverging the flow of people on O'Brien Road footbridge.*

香港的天橋充分發揮了時間和空間的化學作用，創造出奇特的畫面，也提高了速度和效率。東區走廊的北角段，它令港島東西兩端的行車時間大大縮短。*The flyovers in Hong Kong are highly functional and practical with respect to time and space. They help create many peculiar images, and improve on speed and efficiency. The North Point section of the Island Eastern Corridor reduces the travelling time from the west to the east of the island extensively.*

The section of expressway from the Western Harbour Crossing to Cheung Tsing Tunnel, when seen against the old and new high-rise buildings of Mongkok and Sham Shui Po which it passes, seems to be floating adrift in the air. The view from this overpass is totally different from that seen on the ground level. This is really one of the top ten wonders of Hong Kong. The flyover of the former airport also gave the similar kind of cinematic effects.

天橋本來就和速度有關。從天橋上高速行駛的車裡望出窗外，空間快速移動，就像看電影一樣。香港的天橋設計十分簡約，是form follows function，流暢的外形上沒有增添任何多餘的感覺。

Basically, flyovers have a lot to do with speed. When we look out the car window on the expressway, images pass by very fast, and it is just like watching a movie. The flyovers in Hong Kong are in very simple designs, with form following function and smooth appearance without any unnecessary elements.

最可惜的是政府不太會利用橋底的空間，例如由中區到灣仔再連接到東區的東區走廊橋可以變成一個「長廊公園」，讓人看海、跑步、漫步、路上的景觀十分美麗和多層次。

It's a pity that the government does not know how to make good use of the spaces under the flyovers. For example, the space under the Easter Corridor from Central to Wanchai, and Wanchai to the Eastern District, could be turned into a "promenade park"; where people could enjoy the seaview, take a stroll or a jog. The views along the promenade would be multi-faceted and magnificent.

行車天橋關係到速度，行人天橋就是結合時間與空間的經驗。中區半山的行人天橋，呈現時間和空間的流動經驗，可惜其設計十分「平庸」，不經典，不現代，也不輕盈。好看的是四周的環境，超高密度的新舊高樓，像植物一樣從地上生長出來，高高低低，大大小小，有不同顏色和不同物料的質感。

Flyovers for cars are closely related to speed, while footbridges are the combined experience of time and space. The Central-Mid-Levels escalator and walkway is an experience of moving along with

中區恆生銀行總行的建築，設計特色延伸到連接中區行人天橋系統的橋段上，令整個天橋系統每一段都有不同的個性。*The design of the Hang Seng Bank Headquarters in Central extends to the footbridge of the Central Elevated Walkway system, enabling each section of the entire walkway system to have its own characteristic.*

time and space. It's too bad that the design is very "mediocre", not classic, not modern, and not delicate and graceful. What is good about it is the surrounding environment, with a high concentration of old and new high-rise buildings, like large and small plants growing out of the ground climbing up, high and low, in different materials in various colours and textures.

　　最繁忙的香港行人天橋應該是灣仔地鐵站開始至告士打道政府合署的一段，由上班時間開始就是截不斷的人流，又經常有人在派傳單，做問卷調查，是香港特色的公共空間。在橋上看軒尼詩道的汽車流動，隨時可見由二十多部巴士組成的「火車」，填滿整條大路，巴士像一節節火車卡一樣緩慢地移動，的士小巴則像昆蟲在當中穿插。The busiest footbridge in Hong Kong should be the one stretching from the Wanchai MTR Station, across Gloucester Road to the Government Offices. During rush hours in the morning, there is a constant flow of pedestrians, with people handing out leaflets, doing surveys with questionnaires. It is a public space with very distinct local characteristics. If one looks down at the cars running on Hennessy Road, one can easily find the kind of "train" formed by 20 odd buses in a line any time of the day. These buses fill the entire road and move forward slowly like train carts, while taxis and mini-buses are like insects squeezing their way through.

香港高樓大廈多，又十分密集，天橋成為非常好的觀景台以及連接平台，看香港不單可以在地面看，也可以從天橋的不同高度，不同角度看，十分立體，感受不同的生活和社會空間。中環區的天橋的特色就是冷氣開放，把不同的大廈和高樓連接起來，置地廣場、太子大廈、交易廣場、文華酒店、歷山大廈、渣打銀行等等建築被冷氣天橋連接起來而成為超級建築。

There are many high-risers in Hong Kong and they are densely clustered, and so flyovers become very good viewing and connecting platforms. One can view Hong Kong not only from ground level, but also from flyovers with different heights in different perspectives. It is a very multi-dimensional perception, experiencing different lives and social spaces. In the Central District, the distinguishing feature of the flyovers is air-conditioning. The tall buildings and towers like the Landmark, Prince's Building, Exchange Square, Mandarin Hotel, Alexandra House and Standard Chartered Bank, are all connected by air-conditioned flyovers, turning them into one big superstructure.

香港島的天橋比九龍多，九龍常見地底隧道，好處是街道的景觀不會被截開，像連接旺角與尖沙咀的彌敦道就可以像紐約的大街一樣用作大型花車巡遊，或用作每年的馬拉松起跑，可以是十分壯觀。

There are more flyovers on Hong Kong Island than in Kowloon. Meanwhile, underground tunnels are common in Kowloon, and the good thing about them is that the roadscape would not be truncated. Let's take Nathan Road as an example, it connects Mongkok to Tsim Sha Tsui like the avenues in New York City running through the metropolis, with spectacular events taking place like the Thanksgiving Day Parade and the Marathon.

灣仔軒尼詩道修頓球場一段，巴士來往多而密，巴士超長的車廂，一輛接一輛的就像火車卡相連着。The traffic on Hennessy Road in the Southorn Playground section in Wanchai is usually heavy, with many buses running through. Most of these buses are long, and they form a kind of "train" with one moving slowly after another.

地下鐵
»The Underground (MTR)«

人們都愛説香港是個沒有歷史意識的城市。

People love to say that Hong Kong is a city without historical consciousness.

高樓大廈旋生旋滅，城市慢慢失去了新與舊互存的特色。

High-rise towers come and go, the city is gradually losing its special trait of coexistence of the old and the new.

我們會讚嘆倫敦、俄羅斯的地鐵站和火車站怎樣宏偉，巴黎地鐵的新藝術設計字款怎樣美觀。

We are amazed by the grandeur of the underground and train stations in London and Russia, and appreciate the beauty of the Art Nouveau letters of the Paris' Métropolitain.

至於我們每乘搭的香港地鐵呢？

But how about the MTR[1] that we ride on everyday?

香港眾多公營機構中，最具設計風格意識的首推地下鐵路，而它的設計美學風格也是最統一的。與其他國際大都會如東京、巴黎、倫敦、紐約比較，香港的地鐵特別整齊明亮。設計理念就是form follows function，美學就是簡約主義。心思都花在顏色、燈光等營造空間質感和功能效率至上的元素上。

Of all the public sector organisations in Hong Kong, the one with the best consciousness in design style has to be MTR. Compared with the subway of other big cities such as Tokyo, Paris, London and New York, the MTR in Hong Kong is particularly clean and bright. Its design concept is form follows function, the minimalist aesthetics, where thoughts are put in functional elements such as colours and lighting to create a sense of space and efficiency.

1.MTR (Mass Transit Railway), equivalent to the subway, underground or metro system of other cities.

地鐵東涌站的設計具備都會車站氣派，明亮、簡約、高大的空間就像願望，香港人應感到驕傲。The design of Tung Chun MTR Station is impressive with so much style, just like other cosmopolitan metro stations. It is bright and minimalistic, and has spaces with curves and circles, giving a strong sense of sculpture. It is a design Hong Kong people could be proud of.

流動風景
Moving Scenery

香港第一段通車地鐵是由九龍塘至觀塘，當時是上世紀八十年代初期，大部分人都是以巴士或小巴代步，我仍然記得每天上課都乘1A線由尖沙嘴到坪石的巴士以人售票的日子。

The first MTR line to run is that of Kowloon Tong to Kwun Tong, opened during the early 1980's, when most people still relied on buses and mini-buses . I still remember the days when I took bus number 1A to school, from Tsim Sha Tsui to Ping Shek, when there were still "bus conductors" selling tickets on the buses.

地鐵出現以後，把城市的空間、時間觀念改變了。記得八零年讀初中時第一次到九龍塘試乘地鐵，感覺有點像小說《百年孤寂》裡小鎮人物第一次看見冰的神奇感覺。由購票過程開始，到月台、踏進列車，車卡在運行，列車在架空橋走的時候，看着外面的風景和建築物的流動，像走進了一個太空基地……這些經歷加感覺都是由各種不同的設計營造出來的。

Since the running of the MTR (Mass Transit Railway), the perception of space and time in the city has changed. I recall the first experience of riding on the MTR from Kowloon Tong Station, the feeling was like the miraculous sensation of the folk in a small town when they saw ice for the first time in the book "One Hundred Years of Solitude". All the steps from buying the ticket, walking along the platform and getting into the train, and the train in motion, seeing the scenery and buildings flowing by while the train went along the flyover, it was just like being in a space station…, all the experience and impressions were created by the various designs.

地鐵由小小的一張車票、售票機、大堂內部空間、空間裡的標誌與顏色組合，月台查詢/補票站、廣告燈箱的大小及不同站名名稱和字體運用，都是經過詳細思考才設計出來。像港島站採用了中國書法作為字體，是典中西合璧的成功例子。紙皮石是主要內部空間的材料、每個站都有自己獨特的主色、月台上小小的服務站是玻璃加不鏽鋼構成的一個小盒子……都是各個地鐵站的基本功。

Every component and detail of the MTR such as the ticket, the ticket vending machines, the lobby interior, the compositions of colours and signs, the information booth, the advertising light boxes, as well as the Chinese characters of different names of the stations, all are products of design with meticulous thoughts. For example, the station names along the Hong Kong line were written in Chinese calligraphy, which is a successful case of integration of east and west. Mosaic is used as the major material of the interior, and every station has its own colour or colours, the service booth at the platform is a little box of glass and stainless steel... these are the basics of each station.

　　各站繼而在基本功上再進一步，荃灣線架空路段最富電影感，列車駛過架空部分，就像電影在運用推軌鏡頭一樣。位於高樓大廈之間、架空橋之上的荃灣車站，由於沒有空調，樓底又比較高，與其他位於地底的車站空間有強烈的對比。

A step advanced from the basics, the view of the elevated section of the Tsuen Wan line is strongly cinematic. When the train passes through the elevated tracks, it is just like a tracking shot in the movies. The Tsuen Wan station is located among high-rises with an elevated platform. Since it has no air conditioning, and has a relatively high floor-height, it gives a stronger spatial contrast compared to other underground stations.

閱讀都市
Reading the City

　　觀塘線由彩虹站到觀塘站的架空段是另一部電影，雖然都是高架橋，但不是荃灣線那種密封式。月台是流動的空間，可以看至外面的樓宇風景，材料的主題除了是紙皮石外就是簡約主義常用的石屎平面。

The elevated section of Kwun Tong line from Choi Hung station to Kwun Tong station is another film. Although it is also elevated, it is not of the same closed system as that of the Tsuen Wan line. The

地鐵不同支線車站的字體運用各有特色，是設計者的心思。舊支線通車至今已二十年，但仍未覺得過時。*The choice of font and colour/s for each station along the different lines shows the special characteristic of each station. The choices were made by the designers with meticulous thoughts. The old lines have been running for more than 20 years now, and yet the designs still look fresh.*

platform is a flowing space, with views of surrounding buildings. In terms of materials, besides the typical mosaic, there is bare-face concrete that is frequently used in minimalist designs.

香港的都市空間「十分立體」，在不同的位置角度會看見不同的面貌，這些都是高度密集高樓建築的成果。

The urban space in Hong Kong is very "three-dimensional"; one could have different views from different positions and perspectives. This is the result of the architecture of high-density towers.

地鐵在這些空間的流動提供了閱讀香港都市空間的另一種可能：是速度和多層次角度的結合，形成了香港獨有的都市經驗。

Moving space such as the MTR has provided another reading to the urban space of Hong Kong: it is a combination of speed and multi-level perspectives, creating an urban experience that is particular of Hong Kong.

近幾年地鐵開始利用車廂和車站不同的空間作廣告用途，有人批評這種做法破壞了地鐵的完整性，但這些廣告有時也會產生新的互動。比較成功的是年前索拉奇藝坊的廣告，人物造型在車廂內外展示，既富動感又能構成故事。其實地鐵的廣告空間也可以變成一種「公共藝術空間」，功能不是賺錢，而是提供一種新的經驗，視覺的、聯繫的。地鐵月台也是進行聲音裝置的好地方，像東涌線的香港站大堂，這個三層樓高的「通道」，都是進行各種不同公共藝術活動的理想空間。

In recent years, the MTR started to utilise train compartments and different spaces in the stations for advertising purpose. Some criticise that it is destroying the uniform quality of MTR. However, these advertisements could produce a new interactive dialogue at times. One of the more successful examples would be the promotional campaign of Cirque du Soleil, displaying their circus characters inside the train compartments, creating dynamic effects and a sense of story. In fact, the advertising space in the MTR can also become a space for public art. The purpose is not profit making, but to provide a new visual and interconnected experience. The train

東涌線香港站樓底很高，是簡約設計的風格，令牆上的藝術品更加突出。
Hong Kong Station of the Tung Chung Line has a very high ceiling. It is in the style of minimalist design, and the artworks on the walls are exceptional.

荃灣線是高架橋，列車在高樓大廈之中穿梭，望出車外是一種流動風景，像看電影一樣。The Tsuen Wan Station is located among high-risers with an elevated platform. When you look out of the window riding on the train going through that station, you'd see sceneries flowing by, just like watching a movie.

各車站內的查詢補票站都是玻璃與不鏽鋼物料構成，車站設計既有統一性，亦有差異性。*All information and ticketing booths are constructed with glass and stainless steel materials. All stations share some common basic elements in their designs, while keeping some variations at the same time.*

platform would be a good site for sound installation. For example, the three-storey high circulation space in Hong Kong station of Tung Chung line would be ideal for all sorts of public arts activities.

地鐵生活
The Life of MTR

　　地鐵不限於作為交通工具，也是體驗生活的場所和空間。東涌線的獨特之處是引進「作者論」的設計模式，不同的站由不同的人負責設計，每個站雖然保留簡約的基本風格，但容許不同的發揮。像東涌站就不再只是九十度角的面面直線，空間感有圓有彎，雕塑感特別強烈，這些都是香港設計風格的優良傳統，應多加研究、表揚和發揚光大。

The MTR is more than public transport. It is also a venue and space to experience urban life. The Tung Chun line was drawn up with an "auteur" concept, with each station designed by a different designer. In this manner, the stations maintain the basic minimalist style, while allowing the playing with different ideas. Take the Tung Chun station as an example, it breaks away from the right angle flat surface and has spaces with curves and circles, that gives a strong sense of sculpture. These are the fine traditions of Hong Kong design style, and they should be studied, appreciated and advocated.

近幾年香港人常常在質疑自己的身份認同，總覺得香港沒有甚麼代表，其實任何能夠在香港存在的就是香港的一部分。多留心觀察，就會發現香港其實是個大寶庫，衣食住行都有其性格特色。地鐵是香港的特有產物，香港人卻「身在福中不知福」。地鐵是香港人集體情懷的一個重要部分，由廣告到車站設計，都在影響着香港人的生活習慣與生活價值；只要用心研究背後理論和創作方法，分析其影響，就是歷史觀的體現。

In recent years, people of Hong Kong always question themselves about identity, and always think that there isn't anything representative of Hong Kong. Actually anything that exists in Hong Kong is a part of Hong Kong. When one pays more attention, one would find Hong Kong is actually a treasure chest; and there are very special characteristics in each and every aspect of our daily life. The MTR is a very special product of Hong Kong, but people in Hong Kong do not realise how fortunate they are. MTR is an important part of Hong Kong people's collective memory, from advertising to station designs. It is shedding influence on our habits and values. Should we study carefully the theory behind, its creative process, and analyse its influence, then, it would be a realisation with a historical perspective.

香港國際機場
»Hong Kong International Airport«

香港國際機場有點像一個歐洲式的大型火車站，總是人頭湧湧，從不冷清，不似某些機場，偌大的空間，有時冷冷清清，冷得有點像科幻片電影裡的場景。

The International Airport of Hong Kong is somewhat similar to some big European train stations. It is always filled with people and never quiets down, unlike some other airports that would become quite empty and quiet at times that they seem like a set for a sci-fi movie.

香港的機場建築設計也像一個火車站，巨大的屋頂把所有東西覆蓋起來。它的空間感十分強烈，也是香港政府建築裡另一能達到國際水平的設計。負責建築設計的是中環匯豐銀行總行的建築師Norman Foster，他是近三十年來國際上最具影響力的建築師之一，其作品遍佈世界各地，但中環的匯豐總行是他建築師生涯最重要的轉捩點，也是所謂 High-Tech（高科技）派建築得成正果的重要作品。

The architectural design of Hong Kong's airport is also like a train station's, with everything covered with a huge roof. With its strong spatial quality, it is one of the few public projects that reach international standard in design. The architect responsible for the airport is Norman Foster, who is one of the most influential architects in the last thirty years, and who has also designed the HSBC Headquarters. His projects can be seen worldwide, and the HSBC Headquarters is a crucial point of his career as an architect, as well as an important product of the High-Tech school of architecture.

Norman Foster 像其他現代主義信徒那樣，深信建築和機器設計一樣，應該由「功能」開始，不需要有多餘的裝飾。當然，所謂從「功能」出發，人人對功能的演繹和看法也不一樣。

As other Modernist designers, Norman Foster believes in designing architecture as machines, and focus should be on "function" without

由 Norman Foster 設計的新機場絕對是香港的地標建築之一，更屢獲國際殊榮。但廣州新白雲機場落成後，亞太地區的樞紐機場重新「執位」，當局務必要審慎部署，鞏固世界物流中心的地位。 The new airport designed by Norman Foster is definitely one of the landmarks of Hong Kong, and it has won international acclaim and prestigious awards. But after the completion of the new Guangzhou Baiyun Airport, there would be a reshuffle in the choice of a hub airport in the Asia-Pacific region. Our authorities should be prudent in their strategies to consolidate Hong Kong's competitive advantage as a leading global logistics hub.

excessive decorations. Certainly, everyone has a different definition and interpretation of "function".

　　像香港國際機場的設計，重點是表達空間的偉大和統一，功能是配合航運這個特大空間，但設計上有一些功能上的嚴重缺點，第一個最明顯的敗筆是洗手間的設計。洗手間的空間過分狹小，根本不配合一個大機場的需要，而洗手間對乘搭飛機的乘客來説是極為重要的。As such, the emphasis of the design of Hong Kong's International Airport is to express the magnificence and unity of space, and to function as an extra-large space for aviation. However, there are still some serious functional faults in the details, the first and most obvious one would be the design of the restrooms. The restrooms are tiny, and that can hardly cope with the needs of a large airport, where restrooms are extremely important to passengers.

　　而另一個缺點就是內部遊走的「路途太遠」。如果在六十號閘口下飛機，要走一段很長的路才能到達機場鐵路，但這是單方向流動設計上的必然效果，原因是香港機場的其中一個設計概念，是希望能夠透過一個平面、一個方向，來解決所有人的流動。

Another fault is the internal circulation distance being way too far. If you get off the plane at gate 60, it would take quite a while before you arrive at the airport express train. This is the inevitable outcome of a single-direction circulation design, for one of the airport's design concepts is to solve all circulation issues through one level and one direction.

　　正在進行的機場擴建和重修工程是必要的，但新的設計似乎不夠簡潔，尤其是指示牌十分混亂。然而，香港機場最失敗的是食店素質差劣，香港是美食之都，機場的食店應反映香港這方面的強項，現在竟然大量生產劣質食物，很是失禮。

The renovation and expansion taking place now are necessary, yet the new design does not seem to be simple enough, particularly the signage system that is very confusing. Anyhow, what is worse about the airport is the poor quality of food in its eateries. With Hong Kong being the capital of cuisine, the restaurants in its airport should live up to its name, but the poor quality of the mass-produced food there now is a total disgrace.

香港是個大商場
»Hong Kong Is One Big Shopping Mall«

　　商場是香港最具代表性的公共空間，不同年代有不同種類的商場，尖沙咀的海運大廈是香港最早期的高級冷氣商場。百貨公司是早期的大型商場，像永安、先施、連卡佛，國貨公司有裕華、中僑。但上世紀八十年代的高地價政策，徹底改變了香港的商場空間。

The shopping mall is the most representative public space in Hong Kong. There are different types of shopping malls at different times. The Ocean Terminal was the first mall in Hong Kong with air-conditioning. Department stores served as the early malls, such as Wing On, Sincere, and Lane Crawford; there are also "Chinese Products Emporiums" such as Yue Hwa and Chung Kiu. However, with the "high land price" policy from the 1980's, commercial spaces in Hong Kong have changed tremendously.

　　首先是傳統百貨公司衰落，超巨型大冷氣商場興起，像太古城、沙田新城市廣場、太古廣場，一個大中庭，配上多層的商場空間，內裡大部分卻是差不多的大型連鎖店，沒有甚麼性格和特色。有趣的是，建於多層大商場上面的，是多幢幾十層高的住宅大樓，這種上世紀二、三十年代的歐洲社會主義現代派建築設計，居然在香港這個資本主義社會開花結果。

First of all, came the decline of department stores, then, the rise of super-large air-conditioned shopping malls such as Taikoo Cityplaza, New Town Centre in Shatin and Pacific Place. They are usually composed of a large atrium with several levels filled with chain stores that are more or less the same, without any distinct identities. An interesting point is that above these multi-level malls, are residential towers of over thirty-story high. Surprisingly, these modernist European socialistic ideal designs blossom in this capitalistic city of Hong Kong.

利時商場的店舖小得不堪，只要有一名客人走進店內，其他人便得站出店外的窄窄通道。 The shops in Rise Shopping Arcade are extremely small, and if a customer walks into a shop, then other patrons would have to stand in the narrow hallway outside the shop.

利時商場的外觀，很難在大街大巷中生存，但它自有其客路。 The exterior of Rise Shopping Arcade is not that appealing, and the arcade can hardly survive on the main streets, but this shopping centre has its own clientele.

超大型商場如尖沙嘴海港城，有一個大中庭⋯⋯⋯⋯二、三十年代歐洲社會主義風格，如今在香港開花結果。 There is usually a large atrium in super large shopping malls, just like it is in Harbour City. It is interesting that this kind of European socialistic design of the 20's and 30's could blossom in Hong Kong.

連通商場樓底較矮，店舖面積細小，但卻是容許小店發展的新商業空間。Winning Shopping Centre has a rather low ceiling, and the shops are quite tiny, but it is a nice place offering opportunities for shop owners to start and develop their small businesses.

百利商場 *Beverley Centre (Tsimshatsui)*
百利商場內的小店，是店主創造自己形象和特色的夢工廠，客人光顧是賞識店主個性的行動。*In Beverley Centre is the dream factory where shop owners create their own images and unique characteristics. People shop there in order to show their appreciation and support for the shop owners' personalities.*

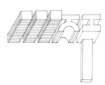

由左至右
From left to right
利時商場：香港九龍尖沙咀嘉蘭圍5 - 11號
Rise Shopping Arcade: 5-11 Granville Ct, Tsim Sha Tsui, Hong Kong
運通商場：香港九龍尖沙咀山林道46 - 48號
Winning Commercial Building: 46-48 Hillwood Road, Tsim Sha Tsui, Hong Kong
百利商場：香港九龍尖沙咀漆咸道南87-105號
Beverley Centre: 87-105 Chatham Rd S, Tsim Sha Tsui, Hong Kong
海港城：香港九龍尖沙咀廣東道3號
Harbour City: 3 Canton Road, Tsim Sha Tsui, Hong Kong

　　七、八十年代香港的物業發展基本都是中小型模式主導，規劃上也是以街道為格局，像尖沙咀一帶就有這種單幢式的樓宇，商場設於地面以上三至五層，運通商場就是一例。特色是樓底十分低，通道十分窄，店的面積十分小，通常都是一些影印舖之類的支援性商店，但這種小商場有時也能成為一種新的商業空間，讓一些具特色的小店發展。

In the 70's and 80's, property development in Hong Kong was mostly medium and small-scale, and the planning was according to street patterns, such as the stand-alone buildings in Tsim Sha Tsui, with shopping malls located on the 3rd to 5th stories, and Winning Commercial Building is an example. Their characteristic is that the floor height is usually quite low, the hallway is relatively narrow, with stores of tiny space, and most stores are generally of supportive nature, such as photocopying shops. These tiny shopping centres became a new type of commercial space, allowing small shops to develop.

香港需要大戲院
»Hong Kong Needs Big Cinemas«

香港有「東方荷里活」之稱，戲院自然多，可惜大戲院在香港已經沒落。雖然經過改建，九龍尖沙咀海運戲院是唯一仍然能令人感受到舊式大戲院氣氛的。現在的海運只佔舊海運超等座位位置的空間，可以想像，海運曾經是一間多麼巨大的戲院！

Hong Kong is anointed as Hollywood of the East, and naturally there are many cinemas here, but unfortunately, big cinemas are in decline. Even after downsizing and reconstruction, the Ocean Cinema (formerly known as Ocean Theatre) in Tsim Sha Tsui is the only cinema that still feels like a grand old movie theatre. The existing Ocean Cinema used to be the balcony section of the former Ocean Theatre. So, you can imagine what a huge movie house Ocean Theatre used to be!

昔日，滿街都是大戲院，如普慶、嘉禾、新聲、麗宮、碧麗宮等。大戲院在上世紀八十年代末開始消失，也就是高地價政策的後果。政府當時沒有保留古跡的政策，很多具歷史文化建築價值的大戲院就此永不復見了。香港因而失去了很多共同記憶和文化旅遊的資源。

In the good old days, there were big movie theatres everywhere in Hong Kong, like Astor, Golden Harvest, Sands, Paris and Palace. The number of big movie theatres started to decrease towards the end of the 1980's as a result of the high land price policy. At that time, the Government did not have any policy for preserving historical structures, and so many big movie houses of great historical and cultural values were torn down and never to be seen again. Many collective memories and resources for cultural tourism were thus lost.

北角的皇都戲院雖然還未拆掉，但已被改建為四不像的商場加桌

北角的皇都戲院雖然還未拆掉，但已被改建為四不像的商場加桌球。
深: State Theatre in North Point is not yet demolished, but it has been
converted into a weird shopping arcade with billiard parlours or poolrooms.

球城，皇都戲院的設計其實十分有特色，屬蘇聯二十年代風格前衛的建構主義作品，非常值得保留。

State Theatre in North Point is not yet demolished, but it has been converted into a weird shopping arcade with billiard parlours or poolrooms. Actually, the design of State Theatre is very special, something close to the avant-garde Soviet Constructivism in the 1920's, something worth preserving.

已經拆卸的舊普慶戲院是昔日左派戲院的龍頭，設計屬史太林古典主義的風格，像北京人民大會堂那種古典簡約，再添上一點點中國民族設計的色彩。

The old Astor Theatre that had been demolished used to be the leading left-wing cinema, constructed in Stalin Classicism style with classical simplicity, similar to that of the Great Hall of the People in Beijing, but with an extra pinch of Chinese ethnic flavour.

土瓜灣的珠江戲院也十分巨型，小時候在那裡看了很多六、七十年代的革命電影，印象最深的是這些電影的色調，像寫實主義的油畫。

Ruby Theatre in To Kwa Wan was gigantic. I saw some revolutionary films of the 60's and 70's there when I was a child, and what impressed me most then was the colour tone of those films that made the images seem like Realist paintings.

現在香港的戲院一點特色也沒有，越來越細，像家庭影院，音響也不理想。

Now, cinemas in Hong Kong do not have any character at all. They are getting smaller and smaller, becoming something like a home theatre, and the audio system is far from ideal.

美國近幾年是大戲院翻生，戲院商投資大量金錢去改善戲院的投影和音響系統，座位設計也十分舒適講究，因此，入戲院看電影再次開始成為美國人的主要文化消費活動。香港人辦戲院，就是缺乏了這種基於真心喜愛電影而產生的誠意和生意頭腦。

In recent years, there is a comeback of large cinema houses in the United States. Investors are spending considerable amounts of money to improve the projection and sound systems of cinemas; and seats are beautifully designed and comfortable. Thus, going to the cinema has once again become a major cultural activity for the Americans. In Hong Kong, investors of cinemas lack this kind of business sense and sincerity which come from a real passion for movies.

家庭影音產品越發達，觀眾對大戲院的需求其實越大，大戲院是唯一能發揮電影力量的空間，讓觀眾享受真正的觀影經驗。

As home audio and video products become more developed, audiences would have a higher demand and greater expectations for large cinemas. Big movie theatres are the only spaces where the true power of film could be put into full play, and where audience could enjoy a real movie experience.

墟市不是經濟是文化
»The Bazaar
is not Economy but Culture«

　　墟市其實是文化遺產和文化產業。成功的墟市通常都具備與宗教、地區民族、種族、社會某階層有關的文化特色。墟市的形成經過時間和歷史的洗禮，像釀酒一樣，年份越久越有特色。

The bazaar (street market) is essentially cultural heritage and a cultural industry. A successful bazaar usually has characteristics related to religion, local or ethnic culture, or certain social strata. A bazaar has to go through baptism of time and history, just like wine, with characteristics growing stronger over the years.

　　其實，香港在上世紀八十年代，仍然存在很多富有歷史和特色的墟市，像旺角的雀仔街、中環的花布街，以及散佈在大街小巷的小型墟市。但兩個前市政局的小販政策，把香港所有富有特色的墟市都差不多消滅掉。當時是泡沫經驗的年代，大家都為財大氣粗的暴發戶心態支配，不懂關心這些香港文化遺產。

In fact, in the 80's, there were still a lot of markets with history and characteristics in Hong Kong. Such as the "bird street" in Mong Kok, the "fabric street" in Central, as well as many smaller bazaars distributed around various streets and alleys. However, two policies of the former Urban Council regarding street vendors destroyed almost all of these bazaars. It was at a time of "bubble economy", and everyone was dominated by the mentality of the new rich, they do not know how to care about these cultural legacies of Hong Kong.

　　近年經濟低迷，政府推出本土經濟概念，本來是個好主意，可惜在執行上欠缺文化修養，只曉得從行政管理角度看事情。推動本土經濟，同時也是在保存香港民俗文化和本土化特色，需要對香港歷史、文化藝術和都市發展有深入的理解，才能對症下藥。現在政府辦的墟市，如上環大笪地，已淪為露天的廉價廣場，沒有性格，沒有做事前研究，完全是典型的反智做法。

The economy is going downhill these recent years, and the government talks about propagating local economy, which is a great idea. However, there is a lack of cultural background on the level of execution, and they look at things only in terms of management efficiency. Boosting local economy is also to preserve local culture. In order to tackle the issue at its source, it is necessary to have a thorough understanding of Hong Kong's history, arts and culture as well as urban development. The current bazaar type activities organised by the government, such as, the Sheung Wan Bazaar has been reduced to a low-price outdoor flea market without character, without prior research, organised in a typical anti-intelligence method.

　　台灣和新加坡政府也有推動墟市。台灣是把社區發展和文化發展連結起來，稱為「社區營造」計劃，是結合了民俗文化藝術、都市規劃，以及建築設計和社區發展的一系列軟體計劃，事前曾進行一系列的研究，定下策略。新加坡地方雖然比較小，但在牛車水唐人街的墟市規劃，也是先經過很詳細的研究的，例如政府透過研究和甄選，邀請了全新加坡最美味的街邊食店遷入墟市營業，概念有點像香港食家蔡瀾先生在香港紅磡黃埔花園的商場所策劃的蔡瀾美食坊。

The governments of Taiwan and Singapore also push for the development of bazaars. In Taiwan, it is considered a "community project", integrating culture with community development. It is a series of proposals with hardware and software, involving national culture and arts, urban planning, architectural design and community development. The policies were set following a series of studies. Singapore is a smaller place, but the China Town bazaar project was devised after detailed studies. For example, through studies and selection, the government invited some of the best street food vendors in Singapore to move in to the bazaar, the idea was similar to that of Choi Lan the food critic in Hong Kong who has developed a "Choi Lan Food Bazaar" at Whampo Plaza.

　　香港有足夠空間發展不同類型的墟市，像二手市場，或以食物、宗教和民間信仰為主題的墟市。但政府要相信「研究」，事前要做好資料蒐集和研究工作。很多人以為創意是天生的，不錯，但最佳的創意來自觀察和研究。香港政府缺乏創意，就是因為不會觀察，不明白研究的重要性。

In Hong Kong, there are sufficient spaces to develop different kinds of markets and bazaars, such as those for second-hand goods, or those with a theme in cuisine, religion or vernacular beliefs. However, the government needs to believe in "researches", and they would need to work on prior studies and information collection. Many would think creativity is inherent. It is true in a sense; however, the best creativity comes from observation and studies. The reason for the government's lack of creativity is that they do not understand the importance of observation and studies.

公共空間不足夠
»The Lack of Public Spaces«

　　農曆年廿九，銅鑼灣的街上填滿了人，維多利亞公園裡的人群有秩序地緩慢移動，但實在太擠了，根本看不到公園裏的年宵市場的攤販在賣甚麼。

Two days prior to the Chinese New Year[1], the streets of Causeway Bay would be filled with people. The crowds inside Victoria Park move around slowly in an orderly manner. However, it is way too crowded, and no one is able to see what are being sold in the stalls of the Lunar New Year Fair in the park.

　　每年聖誕過後，就是新曆新年，而接着的農曆新年應該是香港人的節日高潮。政府近幾年也很努力要加強節日氣氛，卻克服不了一個先天性的問題——香港缺乏大型活動的公共空間，因而所有大型活動都差不多集中在同一、兩個場地舉行。

Every year, following Christmas and New Year would be the Lunar New Year, which is the peak of the holiday season. The government has been trying very hard to increase the festive mood these years, yet, there is one innate problem in Hong Kong which cannot be overcome – we lack public spaces for large scale activities, and therefore most of the large-scale public activities are held at the same few venues which are big enough.

　　其實香港的地理格局十分戲劇性，維多利亞港的兩岸都是巨型的舞台，九龍半島和香港島的海岸線都應闢為海濱公園，作為讓市民享受的公共空間。香港政府從來沒有把香港的公共的空間規劃好，發展商指商場也是「公共空間」，以換取更大的興建面積，但空間的管理權始終屬於發展商。例如銅鑼灣的時代廣場，發展商說戶外的地方是「公共」的，但其管理權是私人的。

---

1. Lunar New Year Fair: a temporary bazaar/ market set up and open for the public three days prior to Chinese New Year.

Hong Kong has a geographic formation which is quite dramatic: both sides of the Victoria Harbour are large spaces. Both the shoreline of Hong Kong Island and that of Kowloon peninsula should be developed into harbour-side promenades, public spaces to be enjoyed by the people. The government of Hong Kong has never drawn up any good plans for the public spaces of Hong Kong. Commercial developers claim that shopping malls are "public spaces" in order to bargain for larger construction area, but the control of those spaces is still owned by the developers. For example, the outdoor plaza of Times Square in Causeway Bay is described by the developer as a "public space", yet the managing right is still private.

　　過年過節，在廟宇舉辦的活動特別多，政府唯一的德政是沒有把香港百多所古廟宇拆掉。這些分散在全港各地的廟宇都是寶貴的文化資產，富有不同的宗教和文化特色，是很好的香港旅遊資源。中國內地的廟宇文化，在文革時差不多被完全消滅，只有香港和台灣仍舊保留廟宇傳統的習俗。香港政府應該做的，是先研究這些廟宇民俗的特色，再配合發展，發揚光大。日本和韓國在這方面十分成功，尤其是日本的廟宇，其舉辦的經常性活動和周邊的市集，都能牽引巨大的文化商業活動。

During festivals and holidays, there are many activities particularly in temples, and the only good policy the government has made is they did not demolish the hundred something ancient temples. These temples in various districts of the city are precious cultural assets, with rich religious and cultural characteristics; and they are great resources for tourism in Hong Kong. The culture of temples in China was mostly destroyed during the Cultural Revolution. Only in Hong Kong and Taiwan are some of these traditional temples preserved. What the Hong Kong government should do is to study the characteristics of these temples, preserve them accordingly, and then promote and foster their development. Japan and Korea are doing quite well in this aspect, particularly temples in Japan, with bazaars and activities being held regularly; and that can induce great impact on cultural and commercial activities.

年前，政府宣佈容許發展商在大嶼山興建冷氣商場，並以吊車系統連接商場與寶蓮寺。冷氣商場內營業的商店千篇一律，毫無特色，只會破壞寶蓮寺的風味。（註：此計劃即現已落成的「昂坪360」纜車及市集。）

A few years ago, the Hong Kong government announced that they had granted the permit to build a large air-conditioned shopping mall on Lantau Island, and would connect the mall with Po Lin Monastery with a cable car system. The shops in the enclosed mall would definitely be the kind of chain stores one could find anywhere else in Hong Kong, without any special traits, and that will only taint the local colours of Po Lin Monastery. (Note: this proposal has now become the Ngong Ping 360 themed Village and Cable Car)

這種發展模式十分落後，不正常，也不理性，卻彷彿已變成了香港一條不可改變的定律。

This type of development model is very out dated, abnormal and ridiculous. However, it seems to have become an unchangeable golden rule in Hong Kong.

香港缺乏大型活動的公共空間，而維多利亞港兩岸，正好成為一個大舞台。 *In Hong Kong, there is a lack of public spaces for large scale activities; and so Victoria Harbour becomes a big performance space.*

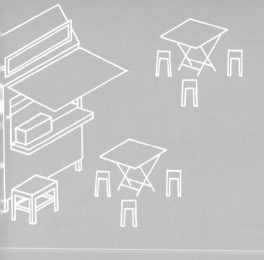

社區的歷史與智慧
The History and Wisdom
of Communities

旺角 Mongkok

物慾基地
»A Playground of Desire«

　　香港的旺角是日本東京的新宿、銀座涉谷、倫敦的蘇豪、紐約的百老匯的混合體，是香港人的慾望遊樂場——砵蘭街、上海街是雲雨交易市場，西洋菜街是民間自發中小企業的大商場。旺角滿足了香港人的所有慾望，知識分子在二樓書店投入人文精神的境界，年青人追逐球鞋潮流、時裝影音產品，發燒友尋找最完美最廉價人氣最新的音響組合，饞嘴的可以吃盡香港的傳統街頭美食。旺角是不可以替代的香港都市文化空間，研究旺角的空間變化和社區歷史，我們會知道更多香港文化的源頭，香港人生活模式和口味的變化歷程。

Mongkok in Hong Kong is a mixture of Shinjuku and Ginza of Tokyo, Soho of London and Broadway of New York. It is a playground of desire for Hong Kong people – Portland Street and Shanghai Street are the market of the "unspeakable trade"; Sai Yeung Choi Street is the mall of medium and small businesses for the average citizen. Mongkok satisfies every desire of Hong Kong people: intellectuals indulging in the humanistic spirit of the "upstair bookstores"; youth following the trends of sneakers, fashion and gadgets; aficionados searching for their dream hi-fi sets with the best bargain; and those who enjoy food can find all the traditional street snacks here. Mongkok is an irreplaceable space of urban culture in Hong Kong. In studying Hong Kong's spatial transformation and community history, we can know more about the origin of Hong Kong culture, the process of the change of tastes and the model of Hong Kong lifestyle.

　　特區政府有意在柴灣成立香港青年發展中心，有朋友提出反對，並指出最貼近年青人的地區是旺角而不是柴灣，每個香港的年青人必定在成長的某一個階段到過旺角，可能是暑假的時候到旺角的漢榮書局買下一個新學期的課本，可能是下課後偷偷的到旺角的小商場買玩具、「四仔」影碟、球鞋，或者第一次拍拖時到旺角看電影，又或者

全新 iA+ 簡易圖像設定 · 創意濾鏡

先達廣場 Sin Tat Plaza

I ♥ HK

Pedestrian Area
行人專用區
All Vehicles Prohibited
所有車輛禁止駛入

旺角 Mongkok

旺角擁有一種有機的美學，雜亂而隨意，街上五花八門，混合着對立與矛盾，是共存共榮的美學。 Mongkok possesses an organic sense of aesthetics. The place is chaotic and random. The streets are full of colours and diversities. It is a mixture of oppositions and contradictions, and aesthetics of mutual existence and shared glory.

第一次想當文藝青年，到二樓書店打書釘……旺角就是香港年青人最巨大的博物館、文化場地、培養生活品味和精神深度的場所。

The HKSAR government came up with an idea to establish a Hong Kong youth development centre in Chai Wan a while ago. Someone against the idea pointed out that the area with the most youth culture should be Mongkok and not Chai Wan. Every teenager in Hong Kong must have hung out in Mongkok at some point of their lives, be it during summer to buy text books for the new semester in "Hong Wing Bookstore", or sneaking out after school to the small shopping centres to buy toys, porn movies or sneakers, watching a movie in Mongkok on a first date, or hanging around bookstores for hours at the first thought of becoming an intellectual... Mongkok is the largest museum, cultural venue, and site to develop a taste for lifestyle or spiritual profundity for young people in Hong Kong.

旺角擁有一種有機的美學，隨着時間和空間而變化的，雜亂而且隨意，混合了草根社團年青人和普通香港人的美學價值觀。街上大大小小、五花八門、五光十色的街招，不覺是概念裝置藝術的色情場所光管招牌……在旺角的美學無關對與錯，混合着對立與矛盾，是共存共榮的美學。這種混合美學是亞洲城市的特色，在東京、台北、馬尼拉都可以找到，但沒有像旺角發展得這樣成熟、多元化和具規模。

Mongkok possesses an organic sense of aesthetics, following the changes of time and space. It is chaotic and random, integrating the aesthetic values of the grass-root young people and the average citizen. Without our noticing, colour street signs of all sorts, signs of erotic venues have become conceptual installation art... the aesthetics of Mongkok is not about right or wrong, it is a mixture of oppositions and contradictions: it is an aesthetics of mutual existence and shared glory. This sort of mixed aesthetics is characteristic of Asian cities. You can find that in Tokyo, Taipei and Manila, but none has developed as matured and diverse as Mongkok.

在旺角的街頭觀察，可以看見很多香港人的故事。不同時段看見不同類型的香港人：下午三時以後是學生，五時以後是下班的白領，或是一家大小，夜晚是遊客和一些好像是社團成員的年青人；乞丐在西洋菜街行乞，警察在追捕疑犯，龍鬚糖師傅在舊樓樓梯底開檔……
都是香港的眾生相。

Observing the streets of Mongkok, one can find many "Hong Kong
stories". There would be different types of Hong Kong people at
different hours: at three in the afternoon there are students; after five
there would be office ladies and families; at night there would be
tourists and young people who look like gangsters, beggars doing
their act in Sai Yeung Choi Street; police chasing suspects, hawkers
with sugar cane candies opening their stalls under the stairways of
old buildings... this is the portrait of Hong Kong.

　　旺角是香港男人性潛意識的投射。香港人在性方面有精神分裂的
特質，不敢在現實世界裡面對的，在「馬檻」和卡拉OK林立的旺角
卻能得到一種滿足，這就是需與求的美學，一個非常有趣的社會學課
題。午夜時分，砵蘭街人來人往，眼睛的視線四處飛揚，洩露了一種
被打壓着的慾望，這就是旺角，香港人的慾望基地，物質生活的完全
場所。

Mongkok is also a reflection of the subconscious of the male
population of Hong Kong. Hong Kong people have a particular spilt
personality regarding sex. They dare not face it in reality, yet their
desires can be satisfied in Mongkok, a place filled with brothels
and karaoke bars. This is the aesthetics of supply and demand, a
very interesting topic of sociology. There is heavy pedestrian traffic
in Portland Street at midnight, with eyes scanning around, with
oppressed desires leaking out. This is Mongkok, the operation base
of desire of Hong Kong, an absolute place of materialism.

文化遺產
»Cultural Heritage«

在外地看見香港旅遊宣傳片，心裡很不舒服。片中的香港就只像外國人眼中的唐人街城市，沒有多少香港人知道的圍村客家人婚宴場面，竟在宣傳片上出現了。

It always makes me feel uneasy watching promo ads of Hong Kong tourism. The Hong Kong in those ads is like China Town in a foreigner's eye. The village wedding banquet known to very few Hong Kong people surprisingly always appears in those ads.

一切感覺很陌生，很虛擬，毫不真實。

All these feel very alien, very virtual, not real at all.

我們不是沒有更有人情味，更有歷史感的生活，而且就在身邊，只是沒有人留意。

It is not that we do not have lives that are more human and more historical, they are actually everywhere around us. It is just that no one has ever noticed.

深水埗是香港眾多舊區之中，仍然保存着大量的老商店、老房子和本地傳統工藝的老社區。

Sham Shui Po is one of the many old districts in Hong Kong where a large amount of old shops, old houses and traditional local crafts still remain.

深水埗一向給人們的印象都不大正派：高登商場的翻版光碟、翻版軟件、鴨寮街一帶的企街鳳姐……治安也好像不太好，既是一個老化社區，也是一個低收入人士的集中地。深水埗好像成為香港這個國際大都會的一個小污點，欲去之而後快。但所謂水清則無魚，有一點雜亂，有一點灰色，生活才有情趣。

香燭紙料 昌興文具紙號

深水埗 Sham Shui Po

在深水埗的大街小巷裏面，有下雨天，有陽光，有風；有着人世間的一切悲歡離合，生離死別，有黑有白有灰有紅有黃有綠。 *In the streets and alleys of Sham Shui Po, there is rain, there is sunlight, and there is wind. There are tears and laughters, there are black and white and gray; red and yellow and green.*

Sham Shui Po always gives an impression that the place is not very decent: pirated CD's, DVD's and software in the Golden Computer Centre, the streetwalkers along Apliu Street... public order here does not seem to be that good either. It is an old community, with a concentration of the low-income class. Sham Shui Po seems to have become a spot of blemish in this international metropolitan of Hong Kong that has to be erased. However, as the saying goes, "there won't be any fish if the water is too clear", and bits and pieces of disorder and gray constitute to the delight of life.

沒有歷史的都市
The City without History

到深水埗散步，尋寶。
Going to Sham Shui Po for a stroll, for treasure hunt.

　　舊式文具店、紙紮舖、玩具店,沿着青山道漫步,像走進香港建築史的時間廊,三、四十年代的典型騎樓底老房子,五、六十年代的工業大廈,七、八十年代的商住兩用大廈,九十年代的高樓,不是甚麼的經典設計,十足十的民間智慧,就是有一點破落的感覺,裡頭的香港,一去不能再回頭,感覺有點淒情、傷感。人們常常說香港是一個不能生根結果的地方,香港人都是過客,所以都不關心舊事物,不相信香港可成為「紐約倫敦」。香港就是香港,一個不需要歷史和情感的城市。過去的事物、過去的感情,我很想保留下來,與下一代分享。

There are old-style stationery shops, stores for paper craft supplies and toyshops in the area. The experience of walking along Castle Peak Road is like that in a time tunnel of Hong Kong's architectural history. There are classical arcade style flats from the 30's and 40's; industrial buildings of the 50's and 60's; commercial-residential mixed-use buildings of the 70's and 80's; and towers of the 90's. They are not any classic designs but simply vernacular wisdom with an impression of being a bit run down. The Hong Kong here is irretrievable once gone, and it makes one feel a bit melancholic and sad. People say Hong Kong is a place with no roots, all Hong Kong people are just passers-by, therefore they would not care about old things. They do not believe Hong Kong can become New York or London; Hong Kong is Hong Kong, a city that does not need history or old sentiments. Yet I really wish to keep these things and feelings from the past and share them with the next generation.

　　在太古廣場、太古城、又一城、新城市廣場以及眾多的冷氣商場,沒有歷史,沒有情感,沒有甚麼可以記憶。商場的光線只有一種,沒有四季,無雨、無風,人與人的距離很接近,卻視大家透明,沒有笑容,沒有甚麼,甚麼都沒有。這就是資本主義唯一的理想生活嗎?

In the many air-conditioned malls of Pacific Place, Taikoo Shing, Festival Walk and New Town Plaza, there are no history, no emotions, hardly anything that is worth remembering. There is only one type of light in the shopping malls; there are no seasons, no rain and no wind. The physical distance between men in these places is very

七層的徙置區、舊唐樓、照相館、露天攤檔，同時出現在深水埗，凝聚了各色人文風貌。 *In Sham Shui Po, you could find seven-storey resettlement blocks, old tenement buildings, picture parlours, and street vendors. It is a melting pot of a heterogeneous society.*

close, but people treat each other as transparent, without a smile, without anything - not a thing. Is this the only ideal life of capitalism?

在深水埗的大街小巷裡，有雨、有陽光、有風，有人世間的悲歡離合，有黑有白有灰，有紅有黃有綠。夏天的汗水，又濕又熱，活受罪。
In the streets and alleys of Sham Shui Po, there is rain, there is sunlight, and there is wind. There are tears and laughter, there are black and white and gray; red and yellow and green. It is hot and humid there in summer, some sort of a living hell.

集體回憶
Collective Memory

記得讀中二那年第一次到高登商場，那兒賣的都是翻版的蘋果電腦、電腦遊戲之類。後來每個星期都會到高登一次，高登是我們當時的博物館和遊樂場，有事沒事都會入去逛逛。高登、黃金代表香港草根的智慧、香港高科技的搖籃、香港subculture（次文化）的土壤。現在的高登和黃金，和以前在精神上沒有太大分別，有正有邪，「三仔」「四仔」，色情暴力，電腦遊戲，漫畫，翻版光碟，應有盡有。香港人在這裡找尋自己的想像，圓滿自己的慾望，這裏是大家的 **Collective Memory**（集體回憶）。

I remember my first visit to Golden Computer Centre was in my second year of secondary school. They sold all sorts of pirated Apple computers and computer games there. Then, I started going there every week. It was our museum and amusement park at that time, and we would go there with or without a reason. The Golden Computer Centre and Golden Computer Arcade are the epitome of grass-root wisdom of Hong Kong. They are the cradle of Hong Kong's high technology, the seedling bed of Hong Kong subculture. They have not changed much in terms of their spirit, there are the good and the evil, X-rated porn movies, sex and violence, computer games, comic books, pirated CD's, you name it, and they've it. Here, Hong Kong people can find their imagination, and fulfil their desires; here is the collective memory of everyone.

　　旺角就是「旺」，人流二十四小時不停，鄰近的深水埗較多空間，多些舊商店留下來，尤其是專門店，像布行及與布相關的大店小店，很多都是寶，世界罕有。旅遊發展局的香港旅遊指南很膚淺，都是老唐人街口味，水過鴨背，不懂得發掘香港的性格。深水埗這個好地方絕對有條件發展深度的文化旅遊，也可以令香港的老事物、舊人情發展下去。

Mongkok is outright "mong" (busy)[1], people streaming along twenty-four hours non-stop. There is more space in the adjacent Sham Shui Po, where more old shops are preserved, especially the specialty shops, such as fabric stores and shops of related trades. Many of them are treasures, one of a kind. "Discover Hong Kong", the tourist guide published by the Hong Kong Tourism Board is very superficial, portraying Hong Kong as an old China Town, skimming through things, without telling the personality of Hong Kong. Sham Shui Po is a good old place which absolutely possesses the quality to develop in-depth cultural tourism. This is also the place that enables old things and old sentiments of Hong Kong for further development.

---

1. The word "mong" in "Mong-kok" means "busy".

潮州老區
»The Chiu Chow Old Districts«

　　香港由小漁村經歷百年滄桑變化，發展成今日的國際大都會，是不斷破舊立新的成果。

With more than a hundred years of transformation, Hong Kong has developed from a fishing village into the international metropolitan of today; this is the fruit of constant innovation by getting rid of the old and bringing in the new.

　　這個不斷「破」的規律，卻將一些值得保存的舊特色一併抹去，令個別社區失去獨特的個性。

However, this pattern of "getting rid of the old" all the time has also erased some old characteristics that are worth keeping, and made some individual neighbourhoods lose their uniqueness.

　　曾幾何時，上環是潮汕人的地頭，今日卻已不成氣候。上環舊區重建以後，原來的潮汕社區接近完全消失，潮州小食店、雜貨店、茶樓、酒家、海味店都不見了。如今，九龍城算是碩果僅存的潮州老區，仍保留了一些典型老香港的騎樓底建築，但不知何時又會被湮沒！

Once, Sheung Wan was the home base of people from Shantou of Chiu Chow origin, although it is no longer the case now. Ever since the redevelopment of the Sheung Wan old district, the original Chiu-Shan (Shantou, Chiu Chow) community has almost disappeared completely. Gone are the Chiu Chow eateries, grocery stores, teahouses, restaurants, and dried seafood stores. Now, only Kowloon City could be considered as the only surviving old Chiu Chow quarters, where some typical old Hong Kong arcade architectures still remain, but no one knows when they will be erased!

已結業的樂口福曾是少數能保持老式設計的潮州酒家，金龍金鳳，可説是中式的 Art-Deco。*Lok Hau Fook (closed down now) is one of the very few Chiu Chow restaurants that maintain the old style design – with golden dragon and phoenix, high ceiling – details typical of Chinese Art Deco.*

　　九龍城在舊機場旁邊，所以都是舊式低層樓宇。這裡跟潮州飲食有關的店，如餅店、海味雜貨店、茶樓、老字號也特別多。

Since Kowloon City used to sit next to the old airport, thus, all buildings there are old style low-rise ones. There are numerous shops relating to Chiu Chow cuisine, such as bakeries, dried seafood grocery stores, teahouses, and old brand names.

　　杜琪峰的電影《鎗火》，結局的那段戲，就是在樂口福拍攝。樂口福是少數能保持老式設計風味的潮州酒家——金龍金鳳，高樓底，入口旁邊是掌櫃——是中式的 Art-Deco。

The last scene of the movie "The Mission" by Johnnie To takes place in Lok Hau Fook[1]. Lok Hau Fook is one of the very few Chiu Chow restaurants that maintain the old style design – with golden dragon and phoenix, high ceiling, shopkeeper's counter next to the entrance – details typical of Chinese Art Deco.

1. Lok Hau Fook (樂口福): one of the few remaining old-style Chiu Chow restaurants.

另一家仍然保留一九六零年代設計精神的老潮州酒家，就是尖沙咀星光行的金島：內部設計、食物、接待處都沒有太大的變化；先來一盆功夫茶、熱毛巾……仍是地道的舊式潮州風味。

Another Chiu Chow restaurant that has kept the design spirit of the 1960's is the Golden Island Chiu Chow Restaurant at Star House in Tsim Sha Tsui: the interior design, menu and the reception have not changed much over the years. The restaurant still serves customers tiny cups of "Kung Fu tea"[1] and hot towels for refreshing them... it is the local old Chiu Chow custom.

九龍城另一家老字號是創發，設計風味比較「草根」，主題是明亮的白光、潮州打冷，食物有不同的肉類和海鮮，九肚魚、紅衫魚、鱠魚、大眼雞、滷水鵝、豬大腸、大地魚、紅腸等等，煞是一種奇景。

Another established old name in Kowloon City is Chong Fat, with a design style that is more grass-root. The interior is themed in bright white light for Chiu Chow "da leng"[2]. On their menu there are many different kinds of meat and seafood like fish, goose, pig intestines, sausages, all displayed behind a glass case, and it is such a spectacular sight.

九龍城還有老潮州餅店。和記隆老餅家，將一眾潮州老鄉都凝聚在一起。潮州的餅食與廣東的不太一樣，月餅就是好例子，款式比較多，味道比廣東的清淡。潮州的花生糖也是一絕，以前都是小販在街上賣的，現在澳門還有這種花生糖小販。

There are also old Chiu Chow bakeries in Kowloon City. The long-established Woo Kee Lung Bakery has gathered the Chiu Chow old folks together. Chiu Chow pastries are quite different from the Cantonese ones, take the moon cakes as an example, there are more varieties in Chiu Chow moon cakes, and they have a lighter taste than the Cantonese ones. . The Chiu Chow peanut candy is also a specialty; they used to be sold by street vendors, now there are still some of these peanut candy hawkers in Macau.

---

1. Kung Fu Tea (功夫茶): very strong tea to wake up the taste buds.
2. Da Leng (打冷): the late-night dinner that is a custom of the Chiu Shan people.

説到小販，以前的九龍城寨就是一個潮州小食城，有很多不同的小型食物工廠，大部分都與潮州食品有關。除了食物，以前潮州戲班也是在城寨之內。城寨消失其實是香港社會的損失，城寨是很有特色和歷史意義的一個建築群，也是一個非常獨特的社區，本來密密麻麻的建築群甚具意義，整片夷平了，相當可惜，新建成的寨城公園，太人工化了。

Talking about street vendors, we have to mention that the Kowloon walled-city was previously a Chiu Chow snack town. There were many different small-scale food factories; most of them were related to Chiu Chow food products. Other than food, there was also the Chiu Chow theatre troupe in the walled-city. The demolition of the walled-city is a loss to the society of Hong Kong. The walled-city was a cluster of structures with character and historical significance, a very unique community. The once tightly packed architectural cluster was very interesting and bore great significance. What a pity to raze it to the ground, moreover, the newly built Walled-city Park is way too artificial.

香港的空間，大都十分「小器」。九龍城附近的舊啟德機場樓底高，在香港十分少見，極像一九八零年代的香港，平平整整的設計格局，是「功能」主導而不是「美學」主導。舊機場變成了一個奇怪地方，離境大堂現在是個娛樂城，有小型賽車場、電子遊戲機中心和保齡球場；而二手車中心，在舊機場高樓底的配合之下，視線和比例比較闊，反而有「大器」的感覺。

Most spaces in Hong Kong are quite "petty". The old Kai Tak Airport near Kowloon City had a tall floor height, which is very rare in Hong Kong. It looked like something in Hong Kong in the 1980's, with a flat and square design organisation, led by "function" and not "aesthetics". The old airport has now become something very odd. The former departure hall is now an entertainment complex, with a mini-race course, a computer game centre and a bowling alley. In contrast, there is also a second-hand car lot, standing against the tall floor space of the old airport, its vista and proportion are relatively wide, giving a "grand" impression.

九龍城和記隆潮州老餅家，將一眾潮州老鄉都凝聚在一起。*The long-established Woo Kee Lung Bakery in Kowloon City draws the Chiu Chow folks together.*

在九龍城散步，看看老建築和老商店，總感到很強的破落感，好像很快就會消失。機場搬了以後，九龍城逐漸會有巨大的變化。那麼應該如何變？變成一個個大型屋邨？我看還是應該把這些老建築保留下來，再重新發展為一個潮州飲食文化區，有小食、有精品、有新有舊。

Strolling in Kowloon City, looking at the old architecture and shops, always gives one a strong feeling of disrepair, and it seems the place will vanish very soon. Since the removal of the airport, Kowloon City has been facing tremendous changes. So what should be the changes? To become a series of large residential estates? I think we should rather preserve this old architecture and redevelop it into a Chiu Chow cuisine cultural district, with foods and goods, with the new and the old.

舊區重建對香港很重要，可重新界定香港的身份。高地價的發展模式並不適合，經濟上也行不通，只是香港政府總有一個拆樓的心魔，甚麼都要拆。

The redevelopment of old districts is very important to Hong Kong, and it can redefine the identity of the city. The high land price policy model of redevelopment is not appropriate, and it does not work in economic terms. There is the devil of bulldozing in the heart of the Hong Kong government, with a mindset of knocking everything down.

桑拿浴室
»Saunas and Public Baths«

「桑拿」是北歐的一種傳統，流傳到香港便從外文的「sauna」翻譯為「桑拿」，也可以稱為「芬蘭浴」。香港最古老的澡堂是浴德池，從上海傳過來；香港的桑拿則是自己的發明，設計也十分香港。

"Sauna" is a northern European tradition. When it came to Hong Kong, the foreign word "sauna" is translated into Cantonese characters "Song La" (桑拿), or referred to as the "Finland bath". The oldest public bath in Hong Kong is Yuk Tak Chee[1] that came from Shanghai; and the saunas in Hong Kong are our own invention with a very "Hong Kong" design.

浴德池不是桑拿，但近年「日久失修」，管理和服務開始老化，有一種故事即將完結的味道。若把浴德池按原有的老上海設計特色好好重修，並改善服務模式，將變成一盤十分有吸引力的生意。曾幾何時，浴德池是日本男性遊客的必訪之地。

Yuk Tak Chee is not a sauna but a Shanghai-style bathhouse. Over the years, with poor maintenance, it is now in a state of decrepit. The management and service are also aging, giving an impression of a finale. Should it be renovated while keeping the original Shanghai style characteristics and with service being improved, Yuk Tak Chee could become a very appealing business. Yuk Tak Chee was once a must-see spot for male Japanese tourists.

現時香港桑拿的設計，以舊美麗華酒店地庫的浴龍館最經典，簡約古典。柯士甸道的碧濤澗和新世界酒店未改營之前也有相似的簡約味道。

The Yuk Long House in the basement of ex-Miramar Hotel is regarded as design classic of current saunas in Hong Kong, with a minimal classic style. Pak To Kan at Austin Road and the New World

---

1. Yuk Tak Chee (浴德池): the first Shanghai-style bathhouse in Hong Kong, best known for its celebrity clientele and strict bathhouse tradition. It was closed in Oct 2006.

Hotel before renovation has a similar minimal taste.

　　香港在上世紀八十年代開始富起來，在設計美藝的取向上，也由簡約慢慢轉化為追求物料貴重和表現財富的暴發風尚。雲石和古羅馬，前者是指定的材料，後者是指定的設計語言。桑拿結合本地情色事業，成為一門服務性行業。單純以桑拿和按摩為主導服務的已是買少見少，灣仔鵝頸橋駱克道的新瀛宮芬蘭浴是代表中的代表，也是香港老字號之一，設計特色是防火膠板混合雲石的re-mix，有一種本土的樸實風味。

When Hong Kong began to prosper in the 80's, designs shifted gradually from minimalism to a nouveau riche trend of using expensive materials, flaunting wealth, with marble being the appointed material, and Roman the designated design language. Saunas, in combination with the local sex industry, became a service business. There are fewer and fewer places that give purely sauna and massage services now, the New Paradise Health Club on Lockhart Road in Wanchai is the most representational. It is one of the oldest names in Hong Kong, with a Formica sheet and marble remix and a down-to-earth local flavour.

　　尖東大富豪夜總會則是另一個故事。大富豪完全反映了香港暴發文化的精神面貌，設計風格是一種比後現代更後現代的誇張，十足是拉斯維加斯風格的姊妹作，主顏色是金，大量的小黃色，大量的金黃色設計細節，大量的深黃色雲石，大量的「羅馬式」雲石柱，和比例不太正確的羅馬/希臘人物雕像。曾幾何時，大富豪是香港文化的一個代表性符號，在上世紀八、九十年代，對國內同胞來說是個神秘的地方，也是香港財富的一個代表符號，裏面的小勞斯萊斯多次成為新聞的話題。

Club Bboss in Tsim Sha Tsui East is another story. Club Bboss totally reflects the culture of the nouveau riche of Hong Kong. The design style is an exaggeration more post-modern than post-modern, a spitting image of the Las Vegas style. Its main colour scheme is in gold, with a lot of yellow gold, a lot of golden design details, a lot of amber marble, a lot of "roman style" granite columns, and Roman or Greek sculptures in wrong proportions. Club Bboss was once a symbol of Hong Kong culture. In the 80's and 90's of the last century, this place was a mystery to those from the mainland. It was also a symbol of wealth, and the mini Rolls Royce in Club Bboss had become a tabloid topic for many times.

　　美國近代最有影響力的建築師和理論家 Robert Venturi 寫過一本書叫《Learing from Las Vegas》（《向拉斯維加斯學習》），他以拉斯維加斯為例，提出「反作者論」，認為建築本身不僅是現代主義眼中一種單純的設計，也是一種符號，可以影響人們價值觀的影像。大富豪以至香港大大小小的桑拿和夜總會，其實是反映香港文化和歷史的一個骨架，電影《金雞》以此出發，可惜以搞笑居多，找不到既可搞笑又蘊含情和理的香港史詩。而香港情色事業的設計歷史和演變，直接反映香港人美學觀的變化與設計價值觀。

America's most influential contemporary architect and theorist Robert Venturi has written a book, "Learning from Las Vegas". Taking Las Vegas as an example, he brings out the theory of "anti-auteur". He believes that architecture is not just pure design in the modernist's eye, it is also a symbol, an image that affects people's values. Club Bboss and all kinds of saunas and nightclubs in Hong Kong have in fact displayed the framework of Hong Kong culture and history. The two "Golden Chicken" movies also talk about this; unfortunately the movies are mostly farcical, missing the chance of becoming an epic of Hong Kong with laughter as well as profundity. In fact, the evolution of the designs of the sex industry in Hong Kong reflects directly the changing values and aesthetics of Hong Kong people.

　　大富豪是一個很好的研究個案。泡沫經濟爆破後，大富豪已失去了昔日的雄風，冷冷清清的大堂，經過歷史和時間洗禮的空間，暴發式的 over design 突然塗上了歷史的印記。記得曾經有位香港大學建築系同學提出研究香港的情色空間設計，後來被老師否決了，真可惜，香港的情色空間實在有太多故事了。設計反映價值觀——物料的運用、顏色的配搭、設計樣式的細節、功能和美學的關係，直接反映了業主的決策價值和當時社會的面貌。戴上道德標準的有色眼鏡，只會產生偏見和誤解。

大 富 豪 夜 總

NIGHT

WESTERN
UNION 西聯
匯款

クラブ ダイフゴー

CLUB
BBOSS

SS
フ

273 00 273
www.sf-express.com

CLUB BBOSS

尖東大富豪夜總會是典型香港設計的代表作。*The design of Club Bboss in Tsim Sha Tsui East is the epitome of Hong Kong style.*

Club Bboss is a very good case study. Since the burst of the bubble economy, Club Bboss has lost its former glory. The lobby is left cold with very few patrons. In this place baptised by history and time, the over design of the nouveau riche is suddenly tuned down by a historical impression. I remember a school friend in the Architecture Department of HKU brought up the idea of studying the business spaces of the sex industry in Hong Kong. Regrettably, the professor turned down the proposal. There are too many stories in the operating spaces of Hong Kong's sex industry worth telling. Design reflects values – the use of materials, the combination of colours, the details of design prototypes, the relationship of function and aesthetics. All these tell us something about the value judgment of the property owner, as well as the society of the time. When one judges with preconceived norms and moral standards, it would only lead to prejudice and misunderstanding.

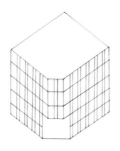

上頁/ 大富豪夜總會：香港九龍尖沙咀科學館道14號
Previous page / Club Bboss: 14 Science Museum Road, Tsim Sha Tsui East, Hong Kong

街道裝置
»Street Installations«

大排檔和街邊小販是民間發展公共空間的好例子，成本低效益高。從設計風格的角度來分析大排檔小販，會發現不同的故事，反映着民間智慧的光明面。

"Dai Pai Dongs"[1] (open space grassroots cooked food stalls) and street vendors are good examples of cost-effective private development of public spaces. If we analyse dai pai dongs from a perspective of design, we shall find all sorts of stories, reflecting the bright side of folk wisdom.

大排檔和街邊小販的消失是近十年的事，是一九八零年代兩個市政局的政策所致。從此香港失去了一種民間風味的都市景觀、旅遊景點。政府常說要創造旅遊景點，治本的方法是放鬆對香港公共空間的過分規管，讓民間百花齊放，發展不同的事物。

Dai pai dongs are disappearing these past ten years, as a result of the policies of the Urban and Regional Councils in the 1980's. Since then, Hong Kong has lost the kind of urban landscape with a distinct folk flavour that is a kind of tourist attraction as well. Our government always says they would like to create more tourist attractions. Actually, the way to go about it is to stop over-regulating the uses of public spaces, and allow various small private businesses to grow and flourish on their own, and diversity would naturally follow.

現在留下來的大排檔大都位於未重建的舊區，中環荷李活道伊利近街附近有兩檔，一檔賣糖水，另一檔賣雲吞牛丸魚蛋粉麵，由一對老夫婦主持。尖沙咀北京道附近天橋底是大排檔集中地，有著名的俊發牛丸和香滑的大排檔奶茶，燒味飯店，炒粉炒麵。

---

1. Dai Pai Dongs (大排檔) : literally it means "big license-plate stall", referring to the special license plate, which is bigger than those of other vendors, issued to each of these food stall owners.

在未重建的舊區，像中環的伊利近街，仍可看到具有特色的大牌檔。 *In old communities not yet redeveloped like Elgin Street in Central, one can still find dai pai dongs with distinctive traits.*

檯椅
Folding Tables and Chairs
檯椅是大排檔的必需品，設計簡單實用，深色的檯面，簡單的結構，到現
在還是香港很多細小間住宅的指定家具。*Folding tables and chairs are
indispensable for setting up a dai pai dong. Their designs are simple and
practical – with dark tops and simple structure. These are still essential
household furniture for many small units in Hong Kong.*

The only dai pai dongs left are mostly in old districts which are not yet redeveloped. There are two near Hollywood Road and Elgin Street in Central, one selling sweet soups (Chinese desserts) and the other selling wonton, fish ball and beef ball noodles, run by an old couple. There is a big concentration of dai pai dongs under the flyover of Peking Road in Tsim Sha Tsui; and there you could find stalls serving fried noodles, various roasted meats, and the popular Hong Kong style milk tea and the famous beef balls by Chun Fat.

設計從功能出發
Form Follows Function

　　大排檔的設計美學完全是由功能出發的即興創作，有點像一艘登陸太空的小飛船，開檔前是一個盒子，所有相關的檯椅和用具都收藏在裡面。「裝飾」性的就是每檔的招牌，有白底紅子，有黑底金字，有鏡底金字。大排檔的餐具也是一種特色，木筷子，竹筷子，藍邊小碟，藍白飯碗，筷子筒……都是消失中的香港風格設計。

The design aesthetics of dai pai dongs is improvisation under the principle of "form follows function". It is a bit like a little spaceship, with all the utensils, tables and chairs all packed inside. The only "ornamental" piece is the sign or big license plate – it can be red Chinese characters on white, gold characters on black or gold characters on silvering. The cutlery and tableware of dai pai dongs are quite exceptional, and they include wooden and bamboo chopsticks, small plates with blue bands, rice bowls in white and blue, and chopstick holders…all these are disappearing designs of Hong Kong style.

　　另外，佐敦地鐵站口外面有一架賣話梅肉、芒果肉、檸檬乾等中國式糖果的小販車，是唯一仍然生存下來的歷史文物。一架斜面的手推車，裡面一格一格的放著不同的涼果，上面是玻璃片或膠片，包裝的啡色紙袋也是香港一絕。

There is a vendor with a hawker cart at the entrance of the Jordan MTR station, selling Chinese candied fruits like preserved prunes, dried

大坑是香港島最具社區感的社區，中秋的舞火龍、八九層高的住宅樓宇組合、小小的街市大排檔、路邊小販、舊茶樓、大樹，大坑是最適合人生活的都市規劃概念。*Tai Hang is the district in Hong Kong Island with the most sense of community. There you can find fire dragon dance in Mid-Autumn Festival, clusters of residential buildings around 8 to 9 storey high, small dai pai dongs in the market, street vendors, old restaurants and big trees. Tai Hang offers the ideal concept of urban planning and living space.*

mangoes, and dried lemons. This cart is a one of a kind surviving historical relic. The cart has a slanting surface, and is divided into many boxes. These boxes are filled with different candied fruits, and covered by glass or plastic lids. The brown paper bags used for packing the sweetmeats are really a classic of Hong Kong style.

香港大坑舊區的兩檔大排檔，賣的是奶茶多士，坐落在兩幢建築物之間的小街，是善用露天空間的好例子。香港的公共空間近年重視的是控制而不是「發展」，警察不容許露天街頭表演，小販管理隊把街頭小販趕盡殺絕，公共空間的功能只是人流的通道，沒有生氣。近年開始推動的行人專用區是好的開始，容許一些空間讓香港的街頭文化重生。

The two dai pai dongs in the old district of Tai Hang serve milk tea and toast. They are situated on an alley between two buildings, and are good examples of making great use of open space. The focus of public spaces in Hong Kong in recent years is on restrictions rather

設於多層街市大廈內的新式大排檔，通風衛生比街頭的大排檔更差。
Dai Pai Dongs situated in a multi-storey market are less sanitary with worse ventilation than those on the streets.

than "development". The police would not allow street performance, and the hawker control team is driving street vendors out of public spaces like criminals, and trying to get rid of them without pity, turning public areas into lifeless spaces of traverse for pedestrians. In recent years, there is a promotion for the concept of pedestrian precinct. It is a good start because from there we could see a chance for revival of Hong Kong street culture.

大排檔一定比露天茶座吸引，種類也多元化。大排檔和小販可把城市裡面的 in-between space 填滿，在香港高樓大廈的環境製造一種「人性化」建築，是街道裝置，是標記（landmark），也是一種社區認同的記憶空間。

Dai pai dongs are definitely a better choice than open air cafes, and their variety is more diverse. Dai pai dongs and street peddlers have taken up the role to fill in the in-between spaces in Hong Kong, a city of high-rise towers, and have given a human touch to our environment. They are street installations, landmarks, and a space of memory acknowledged by the community.

以前西環水街的大排檔，在斜斜的路上一排排的景象已經消失，看着就是不習慣，也會問：好的為甚麼要把它們拆走。

There used to be many dai pai dongs in the slanting Water Street in the Western District. The wonderful sight of rows of food stalls there has disappeared, and I feel something is missing whenever I pass by the spot, and I would ask myself, "Why were they removed? It was nice to have them there."

香港政府把這些香港事物看成毒藥，要把它消滅，理由是難於管理和影響環境衛生。政府以為高樓多層的街市會令衛生更佳就更易管理，其實多層街市比真正的街市更不衛生，通風做得不好，設計不從功能出發，大部分都是設計的反面教材，是座監獄式的政府設計。香港要重拾昔日的風采，精力應花在建立社區空間，啟動民間活力之上，大排檔和路邊小販是非常值得香港人重新開發的事物。

The Hong Kong Government takes these things as pests, and tries everything to eliminate them on the grounds of management and environmental health. They think that putting the market in tall, multi-storey buildings would make it easier to manage and more hygienic. In fact, a multi-storey market is less sanitary than a street market because usually the ventilation is bad due to poorly designed plans which are not function oriented. Most of the design plans by the government are bad, making the market feel like a prison, and they should be taken as negative examples from which we learn. If Hong Kong were to restore its past glory, efforts should be put on establishing community spaces and energising civil dynamics. Dai Pai Dongs and street vendors are things well worth being redeveloped by people of Hong Kong.

冰室世界
»The World of Ice Cafés«

　　每個城市，每處地方都有一種反映其性格的「公共空間」，倫敦是酒吧（pub），巴黎是咖啡座，香港就是「茶餐廳」。

In every city there is a kind of public space that reflects the city's personality. In London there are the pubs, in Paris the cafés, and in Hong Kong there are the Hong Kong style tea restaurants known as "Cha Chan Teng"[1].

　　自從傳統茶樓、路邊大排檔消失，茶餐廳成為香港平民百姓的「公共空間」，古惑仔「講數」、的士司機「吹水」和交換交通情報、白領一邊吃早餐一邊八卦辦公室小道消息……茶餐廳成為小市民小故事的場所。

Since the disappearance of traditional "tea house"[2] and street-side "Dai Pai Dong", Cha Chan Teng has become the public space for the common people of Hong Kong. It is where gangsters "negotiate", taxi drivers chat and exchange traffic info; where office workers gossip while having breakfast... These Hong Kong style cafés are the location for everyday stories of all common people.

　　茶餐廳的「前身」可能是冰室。張愛玲筆下的三、四十年代香港冰室已經絕跡，現在留下來的大都是六十年代開業的，空間設計大都是現代主義（modernism）的簡約風格，又或者是上海二、三十年代最流行的 Art-deco 風格。

The predecessor of Cha Chan Teng would be the "Ice Café"[3]. The ice cafés in Hong Kong of the 30's and 40's as described by Eileen

---

1. Cha Chan Teng or Hong Kong style tea restaurant (茶餐廳): a type of casual dining café common in Hong Kong that provides Cantonese-style western cuisine.
2. Tea House or Chinese restaurant (茶樓): traditional Chinese restaurant that serves dim sum and Chinese tea.
3. Ice Café (冰室): a kind of café which used to be popular in Hong Kong that sells mostly cold drinks and ice-cream.

美都餐室
Mido Ice Café
美都是Art-deco設計的示範單位，也是最值得保留的香港古蹟和旅遊景點。大堂中間橙色底黃色透明膠燈凸字招牌已經在香港失傳，閣樓的一字排開的開揚鐵窗，配合外面公園的大樹，就是最有「香港味」的空間了。*Mido Ice Café could be seen as a demonstration unit for Art-Deco design, and should be preserved as a Hong Kong monument and tourist attraction. The kind of plastic light signage in orange with yellow characters hanging in the middle of the atrium could not be found elsewhere in Hong Kong now. At one end of the mezzanine is a row of iron windows looking out to a park with big trees. This is a space with most "Hong Kong flavour".*

美都餐室：香港九龍油麻地廟街63號
Mido Ice Café: G/F, 63 Temple Street, Yau Ma Tei, Hong Kong

木檯和木椅
Wooden Tables and Chairs

木匠和鐵匠曾經是香港建築工程的前鋒，現在要找一個會「打釘」的木匠也十分困難。美都餐室這木檯腳和全木椅說明了當時香港木匠的手藝和美學品味比現在高明得多，木的質感和線條，再加上時間洗禮、木色變化，所謂歷史感就應該是這樣的。*Carpenters and blacksmiths used to be the vanguards of construction works in Hong Kong, but now it is very difficult to find a carpenter who could handle a nail gun right. This wooden table and wooden chair in Mido Ice Café tell us that carpentry work and aesthetics used to be much better then. The shape and texture of the wood, the changes in colour of the wood with time – this is what we call a sense of history.*

卡位
Booth Seating

卡位是茶餐廳的靈魂，美都的卡位雖然換了幾次，但仍然有一兩張原汁原味的留下來。留意椅腳，原裝是用木加銅腳「打斜」落地，與後來的不鏽鋼腳感覺完全不一樣。*Booth seating is the soul of ice cafés. Though Mido Ice Café has renewed their booth seats for several times, they still keep a couple of the original booth seats. If you look at the legs of the seat, you'd notice that the wooden legs with copper bases of the original seat give an entirely different feel from the stainless steel feet of the new one.*

Chang are all gone, what is left now is usually the ones opened in the 60's. Their spatial designs are usually minimal modernistic, or the art-deco style popular in Shanghai in the 20's or 30's.

過去十多年，這些五、六十年代的冰室或餐室消失得特別快，現在只可以在一些未重建的舊區找到，在深水埗、筲箕灣、土瓜灣、旺角、西環和舊屋邨內艱苦經營。

During the last decade, these restaurants or cafes of the 50's and 60's started to disappear particularly fast. Now, the few surviving ones can be found in older districts where redevelopment has not taken place, such as Shum Shui Po, Shau Kei Wan, To Kwa Wan, Mongkok, the Western District and some old housing estates.

老冰室老餐廳的設計風格，反映了當時平民百姓的美學價值和裝修工匠的手藝特色，像紙皮石、鐵閘、木檯、卡位、燈光裝飾，也反映了那個時代的美學價值，比較着重物料細節及整體風格的統一性。木工、金工、泥水、玻璃的應用和顏色配搭，不是現在那麼粗枝大葉。

The designs of old ice-cafes and restaurants reflect the vernacular aesthetics and craftsmanship of that time. Features such as mosaic, zinc folding gates, wooden tables, booth seats, lights and interior decoration reflect the aesthetic values of that period. A lot of attention was put on materials and details, and the unity of style. The woodwork, metalwork, uses of concrete and glass, as well as the combinations of colours, are not as callously applied as nowadays.

美都到翠華
From Mido to Tsui Wah

以前的冰室或餐室空間感比較強，佈局上大都有一個雙層空間的入口大廳，一邊是收錢的櫃檯，另一邊是玻璃麵包櫃，兩旁是卡位，後面是閣樓和水吧，但高樓價文化下變得不太「實用」。新舊茶餐廳的設計對照，翠華和新釧記的後現代雜亂風格，反映了香港的美學價值由重視物料工藝空間感的以人為本，到現在冷氣主義，只求表面浮華的雜亂意識。

There was usually a stronger sense of space in the older cafes. Their plans are normally a double-height entry atrium, with the cashier on one side and a glass pantry case on the other. Along the two sides are booth seats, and there would be a mezzanine at the back with a bar below. However, these details seem not so "efficient" under the culture of high property price. When comparing the design of old ice-cafes like that of Mido to those of the new cafés, such as the chaotic post-modern style of Tsui Wah or Sun Chiu Kee, one can see the value (taste) of Hong Kong has changed from a humanistic one that emphasises the use of materials, craftsmanship and spatiality to a confused consciousness of nowadays that is flamboyant and superficial, and in which air-conditioning rules.

　　香港電影常常以冰室茶餐廳作為場景，江湖片、愛情片都會找到很多已經消失的茶餐或冰室，這些電影更把這種香港式設計風格影像化為我們對香港歷史和身份的想像。王家衛作品的影像感覺，如《阿飛正傳》、《墮落天使》和《花樣年華》就是很好的例子，若我們把所有香港電影出現過的冰室或茶餐廳片段剪輯下來，細心分析，我們會更了解香港美學價值的變化和香港風格的定義。

Many stories in Hong Kong movies take place in these tea restaurants and ice-cafes. One could find traces of many of these disappeared places in gangster movies or romantic comedies. These movies have transformed this Hong Kong style design into images of our imagination of Hong Kong's history and identity. The impression given by Wong Kar Wai's films, such as "As Tears Goes By", "Fallen Angel" and "In the Mood for Love" are very good examples. Should we collect all the scenes with tea restaurants and ice-cafes from Hong Kong movies, and analysis them in detail, we would understand better the transformation of aesthetic value in Hong Kong and the definition of Hong Kong style.

新釗記是美亂風格的代表。*Sun Chiu Kee is the epitome of new cafés with chaotic style.*

鐵籠萬歲
»Viva Las Cages«

　　政府致力取締僭建物，無視這些僭建「鐵籠」，既有實際功能，也讓住戶建立起單位的特色，其實全港市民都應該享有這樣的生活空間。

The government strives to remove all unauthorised building works, yet they have neglected the significance of some unauthorised "cages". These "cages" serve practical functions allowing the residents to build an identity for their own house. In fact, all people of Hong Kong should be able to enjoy a living space of this sort.

　　最近電視經常播放政府反僭建物的宣傳片：一對情侶在香港的大街小巷遊走，像電腦的RPG遊戲一樣，遭受不同僭建物的襲擊，最後退到一個僭建的露台，當兩人準備相擁一吻的時候，露台便塌下來，屋宇署反僭建物的口號馬上在熒光幕出現。

Recently, there is a commercial for public service played frequently on TV: a couple wandering in the streets of Hong Kong like figures in RPG games, they are then attacked by different illegal structures. Finally, they make it to the balcony in their own home. When they are about to hug and kiss, the balcony collapses, then the slogan against unauthorised building works by the Buildings Department appears on the screen.

　　這種誇大失實的政府宣傳片完全吸收了港產片譁眾取寵的神髓。僭建物是香港建築的特色，政府在近二十年來以安全理由清拆僭建物並無不妥，只是忽視了僭建物對本地民居建築的好處和潛力。

This unreal and exaggerated government propaganda has totally captured the spirit of yellow journalism in Hong Kong movies. These unauthorised structures are characteristic of Hong Kong's architecture. There is nothing wrong with the government taking them apart for reason of safety in the last twenty years, just that they

僭建籠舍是另類的小型空中花園。 *Unauthorised cages are alternative miniature hanging gardens.*

have overlooked the benefits and potential of these structures for the general public.

這些建築物通常以鐵枝作為結構支架,外露於鋼筋石屎的結構之外,其作用主要是把單位面積擴大。

These structures are mostly constructed with iron rods as support, exposed outside of the reinforced concrete facade. Their major function is to increase floor area of the flat.

這些「鐵籠式」僭建物通常用作晾曬衣物、栽種植物、囤積雜物、打麻將、打邊爐等。

These "cage-like" structures are usually used for laundry-drying, as planters or storage, and for activities such as playing mahjong or having hotpot.

從環保角度看,由這些鐵籠製造出來的空間,形成了一個 buffer zone(緩衝地帶),把陽光從室內隔開之餘,也可加強空氣流通,大大減低室內的溫度。

From the perspective of environmental protection, the space created by these cages acts as a buffer zone. Besides blocking direct sunlight into the interior, it also facilitates air-circulation to reduce indoor temperature.

政府近年常常提到空中花園的概念,其實只要望望四周的高樓,當中就有很多由這些僭建鐵籠形成的小型空中花園。在香港密集模式的高樓居住環境下,這些僭建物除了反映「用家」在功能上的需求,也能為單位建立一個 identity(身份)。由鐵窗的設計、鐵籠顏色的選擇、栽種植物的種類,每戶都可以選擇自己的最愛,建立獨特的身份。

In these last few years the government always brings up the concept of "sky garden", actually if we look up at the surrounding towers, there are many mini gardens-in-the-air formed by these cage structures. Under the living environment of super-high density in Hong Kong, these additional structures not only reflect functional needs of the users, but also create an identity for the units. From the design of the metal frame, to the selection of colours and the type of plants put there, each flat-owner could make his own choice and establish a personal identity for his flat.

其實，政府應該修改有關的建築條例，鼓勵市民和建築商以安全和合法的原則，把僭建物正規化。當然，政府作為香港最大的房屋供應商，更應帶頭在公屋實驗這種設計語言。現在香港一式一樣的倒模公屋設計，空間質素像監獄多過像民居。引入鐵籠設計，將幫助空間更綠化和人性化。

In fact, the government should amend the current related architectural regulations, to encourage citizens and builders to formalise those structures in a safe and legal way. Certainly, the government, being Hong Kong's largest property developer, should take the lead to experiment with this design language in public housing. The identical cast-out public housing designs have a spatial quality that makes them more like prison cells than residences. To encourage creative designs for these cages would help make the spaces greener and more human.

香港人把大部分收入花費在住屋之上，竟對居住空間的要求不大，卻熱心大堂有沒有用雲石裝修，屋苑是否有會所，冷氣的普及更減低了大家對環保空間的要求。這些僭建鐵籠正好提供一種對照，一種啟示。

People in Hong Kong spend a large portion of their income on housing, yet they do not demand much of their living space. They only concern whether there is a marble-lined lobby or clubhouse in their complex. Since air-conditioning became widely available, it has further reduced people's demand for environmentally-friendly spaces. These unauthorised cage structures have provided an antithesis, a revelation at the right moment.

空間是人的容器，樓底高一點，就能接觸自然空氣和陽光多一點，看到天空和綠色的樹木多一點，情緒也會改善，看事物也會看得遠一點，待人處事也能更認真。這種生活空間不應該是達官貴人的專利，普通市民也有權利享有。「僭建物」這種香港設計語言，代表了

西方角度
Western Point of View

意大利建築雜誌《Domus》於2001年7月至8月號以香港建築和都市規劃為專題，用西方建築理論分析香港在世界獨有的高密度住宅高樓、僭建物等，對分析香港風格提供了很多參考資料和角度。*Italian magazine on design and architecture, "Domus", did a feature on Hong Kong architecture and urban planning in their July-August 2001 issue. They gave an analysis on the unique aspects of high density of tall residential towers and unauthorised building works in Hong Kong with Western architectural theories. This feature provides a lot of reference materials for analysing Hong Kong style.*

露台與花架
Balconies and Flower Cages

曾幾何時，露台是香港居民的必需品，但在高地價政策和香港政府畸形的建築條例之下，露台差不多成為有錢人的專利。露台的好處多不勝數，心理上減低了細小空間的壓迫感，環保上減低空氣的溫度、促進綠化。花架是露台的一種代替品。上面色彩繽紛的植物，內外看都一樣舒服。*Once, balconies were the basics for Hong Kong residential buildings. But with the high land price policy and the bizarre buildings ordinance implemented by the government, balconies have now become a privilege of the rich. There are so many nice things about balconies – it can lessen the psychological pressure of a small space, reduce temperature and help promote a green environment. Flower cages could serve as substitutes of balconies. With various colourful plants, they are just as refreshing to look at from both inside and outside.*

香港居民的僭建鐵籠有很多用途，晾曬衣服是其中之一。There are many uses of illegal structures like unauthorised cages, and drying clothes is one of them.

民間的多元智慧和平民百姓的生活需要，我們應該好好珍惜，把它納入為「合法」的建築語言。

A space is a container of men, when the floor height is raised then we are in touch with more natural air and light. Being able to see more sky and greens can make our temperament gentler and allow us to view things in a wider perspective; we would also treat other people and things with more sincerity. This type of living space should not be privilege only to the rich and famous, every common joe should have the right to enjoy it. "Unauthorised building works" are a unique element in the design language of Hong Kong, representing the colourful civil wisdom and living essentials of the common people. It is something we should cherish, and to be listed as "legal" and "authorised" in our architectural language.

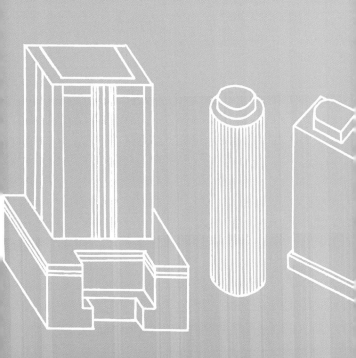

風格的承傳與實驗
The Heritage and Experiments of Style

老酒店風景
»Old Hotels«

　　要發展旅遊業，香港需要更多具有獨特性格的酒店旅館。舊式酒店有很多可供借鏡的地方，因為每一家都努力在設計上和服務上經營出自己的風格，接近歐洲一些旅館。

To develop tourism, Hong Kong will need more distinctive hotels and guesthouses. There is a lot to be learnt from the older hotels, since they all strive to build an identity in terms of design and service, similar to certain European guesthouses.

　　香港的老酒店在上世紀八十年代之後，買少見少。拆的拆，改建的改建，能夠好好保存下來，又不失有風格的，可能就只有文華酒店一家。半島酒店改建以後，以前的歷史感和風味消失了，有點像整形手術做得太好太完美，看上去總有點不習慣。

The old hotels in Hong Kong have been vanishing ever since the 80's. Many of them got demolished or rebuilt. The only one that is preserved without losing its own style should be the Mandarin Oriental Hotel. After renovation, the Peninsula Hotel has lost its touch of history and flavour of the old days. It feels like a plastic surgery done too perfect and too well that one could not get used to the new look.

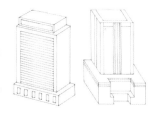

左/文華東方酒店：香港港島中環干諾道中5號
Left / Mandarin Oriental Hotel: 5 Connaught Road, Central, Hong Kong

右/半島酒店：香港九龍尖沙咀梳士巴利道22號
Right / The Peninsula Hong Kong: 22 Salisbury Road, Kowloon, Hong Kong

文華酒店以黑色配搭金色為主調的設計，表現出穩重的氣派。 The design of Mandarin Oriental Hotel is mainly in black and gold, showing sturdiness and pomp.

半島酒店的改造工程雖十分出色，卻因而失去了歷史感和風味。*The renovation of Peninsula Hotel was superbly done, but it lacks style and a sense of history.*

近年改裝的香港酒店，在經營路線上是典型的商務酒店（business hotel），設計上欠缺鮮明性格。以前的老酒店剛剛相反，每一家都希望經營自己的風格——設計上的、服務上的，接近現在歐洲的一些旅館。

In recent years, most renovated hotels turn themselves into business hotels in terms of operation, without any distinctive character in design. In contrast, each of the older hotels hopes to operate in their own unique style in design or service, close to the concept of some hotels in Europe.

經典氣派
Classicism

在高地價環境下經營酒店很困難，尤其是中小型酒店。文華酒店能夠留下來，是因為走高價服務路線。文華的設計風格屬於art deco，沒有半島那種富麗堂皇的大堂，最大特色是顏色的運用，以及空間的佈局，黑色的石檯配以金色的壁畫，細看就知道是一種經過深思的設計語言。金和黑加起來，金的福氣消失了，卻凝聚出一種穩重和經典的氣派。大堂上面的 Clipper Lounge 是香港最舒適的喝茶談話空間。每個客房都有露台，面向立法會大樓的景色特別好。

It is difficult to run a hotel, especially one of small or medium scale, under the high land price policy. The reason why Mandarin Oriental could survive is its classy service approach. Its design style is Art Deco. It does not have the grand lobby of the Peninsula, but its character lies in the colour usage and spatial organisation. From details such as the black granite table and golden mural, one can tell it is a design language with meticulous thoughts. When gold and black are put together, the richness of gold is cancelled out, and is distilled into a dignified and classic style. The Clipper Lounge above the lobby is the cosiest space for tea and a chat in Hong Kong. Each of the guest rooms has a balcony, with a spectacular view of the Legislative Council building across.

1997年曾經傳出文華將重建成一幢七十層大樓的消息。如果成事，論經濟利益當然比現在的大，但從香港歷史文化形象的層面看，就是很大的損失。

In 1997, there was a rumour that the Mandarin Oriental Hotel was going to be rebuilt into a tower of 70 storeys. Should that become real, there would certainly be a greater economic profit than what they have at the present. However, in view of the image and cultural history of Hong Kong, it would be a tremendous loss.

旅遊業的興盛與文化歷史是相連的，曾幾何時香港擁有最多元豐富的歷史文化事物，由西方到傳統中國，由草根到精英，由現代到古典，都可以在香港找到。可惜的是高地價政策推行以後，香港的多元文化景觀漸漸被政府官僚和大財團消磨，越來越單一，權力越來越集中，個人和中小型團體的發展空間越來越小。

The prosperity of tourism of a place is related to its cultural history. There used to be many rich and diverse historical and cultural artefacts and happenings in Hong Kong, from western to traditional Chinese, from grassroots to elite, from modern to classical, all can be found in Hong Kong. Unfortunately, ever since the execution of high land price policy, this diverse cultural landscape of Hong Kong is wearing out by government bureaucracy and the conglomerates, and has become more and more homogeneous. Power is more and more concentrated, individuals and small and medium enterprises have less and less space to develop.

小館風情
The Charm of Small Establishments

文華酒店的設計風格和語言，提供了一種參考的角度，讓我們討論甚麼是風格、甚麼是香港風格。酒店是旅客了解一個城市最密切的空間，香港未來需要更多具不同風格的酒店和旅館，市區重建正好提供了很多機會。

The design style and language of Mandarin Oriental have given us a point of reference to discuss "What is style", and "What is Hong Kong style". Hotels provide the most intimate space for a visitor

銘豐中心
Prudential Centre
佐敦地鐵站上面的銘豐中心，外表有點像太空站，下半部分是商場，上半部分是酒店。矢位和坊間比較有特色和空間感，內部的燈光做得十分有層次，光暗充滿着對比。 Prudential Centre above the Jordan metro station looks a bit like a space station. The upper part of the building is a hotel, and the lower part a shopping mall. The lobby and rooms in the hotel have a nice sense of space and marked characteristics. There is layering in the design of the interior lighting, with differences and contrasts in brightness.

百樂酒店
Park Hotel
尖沙咀漆咸道的百樂酒店外表是十足十的現代主義，簡單的線條，白色淺藍色的配搭，完全有條件 upgrade 成為一間摩登的 boutique hotel。現在的房間仍然保留着上世紀七十年代的氣氛，可能是因樓底比較高吧！*Park Hotel on Chatham Road, Tsimshatsui looks exactly like a Modernist structure, with simple lines and colour combination of light blue and white. There should be no problem to upgrade it into a modern boutique hotel. The rooms still retain an atmosphere of the 1970's – perhaps, it's because the ceiling is relatively high !*

to understand the city. In the future, Hong Kong would need more hotels and guesthouses with different styles, and there are many great opportunities provided by the urban renewal of old districts.

其中一種方法是把一些舊大廈改建成酒店旅館，營運形式可以是家庭式小本經營。新加坡牛車水唐人街區有很多舊樓改建的旅館，規模甚小，風味十足，也是一些獨立旅遊或自助旅遊的人士喜歡的。
One method is to transform old buildings into hotels, which could be run as family-style small establishments. In Singapore's China Town, there are a lot of guesthouses transformed from old buildings, they are small in scale and rich in local flavours, and they are often the preference of independent travellers or backpackers.

離島區流行的渡假屋，其實也很有潛力可發展成具特色的小旅館。政府近年立例規管小旅館，規管過嚴，美其名是保障公眾安全，其實是過分控制，實際得益的是由大財團連鎖經營的酒店，因為只有他們才有足夠行政資源應付政府的官僚程序。
In fact, the popular vacation houses in the outlaying islands have great potential of development into guesthouses with unique characteristics. The government has started recently to regulate small hotels, their over-restrictive rules appear to be for the sake of public safety, yet in reality it is a kind of over-control, with profit going to chain hotels operated by big consortiums, because they are the only establishments to have enough means to deal with bureaucratic procedures.

合和風格
»Hopewell Style«

　　灣仔皇后大道東合和中心、胡忠大廈和海旁的華潤大廈，都是「合和風格」。不合常理的巨大體積、白色的外牆、簡單的幾何形態，啡紅色的大石都是合和風格和特色，沒有裝飾，有點像蘇聯時期建築的簡約版本。有人會覺得冷漠，沒有人味，但與一些典型玻璃幕牆高樓相比，合和風格建築物的面目和身份比較清楚，並成為香港城市空間裡的一種地標，能夠為港人製造集體記憶（Collective Memory）的建築空間。

Hopewell Centre, Wu Chung House, and the CRC Building by the harbour are three structures of a unified "Hopewell Style". Out-of-scale massive structure, white exterior, simple geometric form and brown stones are the signature Hopewell style. Without much ornamentation, they look like simplified versions of soviet constructivism architecture. Some would think the style is too cold and without human touch. However, when compared to typical buildings of glass curtain wall, these "Hopewell style" buildings do have a distinctive character and identity. They become a kind of landmark in the urban space of Hong Kong, architectural spaces where people of Hong Kong create their collective memories.

　　這三幢合和風格建築都坐落港島灣仔，華潤是在灣仔填海新區，合和和胡忠則是在灣仔舊區。灣仔舊區是典型的香港街市格局，小街小巷、小店小販、雜菜水果、豬牛羊雞鴨鵝、海鮮海味、雜貨店、涼茶舖、玩具店、名店、成衣店、地道的香港藝品店，可以找到任何與小市民生活有關的小東西小玩意。在小街抬頭望向巨大的合和中心，感覺特別超現實，它像一條白色的實心圓柱，不經意地落在錯誤地方，成為一個地標（landmark）。在小街小巷迷了路，看見它，就會知道方向，這種地標不可以多，太多就會失去了地標的意義。超大和超小共處一條街道正是香港風格的特色，西方強調的比例協調在香

左/合和中心：香港港島灣仔皇后大道東183號
Left / Hopewell Centre：183 Queen's Road East, Hong Kong Island

右/胡忠大廈：香港港島灣仔皇后大道東213號
Right / Wu Chung House: 213 Queen's Road East, Wanchai, Hong Kong Island

三幢在灣仔的合和風格代表作。胡忠大廈、合和中心及華潤大廈,它們風格統一,白色外牆,簡約設計。*Hopewell Style: The Three Buildings in Wanchai : Wu Chung House, Hopewell Centre and the CRC Building share a unified style – they are massive structures with white exteriors and simple geometric forms.*

華潤大廈外的告士打道像一條河,川流不息地在大廈旁經過。大廈平台最近變身三里屯,side-walk café、酒吧、食肆進駐,人流雖然不多,但有自己風格。 *Gloucester Road outside the CRC Building is like a river, with streams of cars flowing along. The terrace of the CRC Building is recently turned into a new community space, Sanlitun, with side-walk cafés, bars and restaurants. It is not a busy place, but it has its own style.*

華潤大廈:香港港島灣仔港灣道26號
China Resources Building 26 Harbour Road, Wanchai, Hong Kong Island

港完全用不着，高密度的都市空間，高速的建築物新陳代謝，令香港這都市呈現出拼貼風景。

These three buildings are situated in Wanchai of Hong Kong Island: the CRC Building is in the new reclamation area of Wanchai, while Hopewell Centre and Wu Chung House are in the old district. The old district of Wanchai runs typically like a Hong Kong market: with small streets and alleys, little shops and street vendors, fruits and vegetables, meat and poultry, seafood and dried goods, grocery stores, herbal tea houses, toy shops, brand-name boutiques, garment outlets, shops of local crafts... One can find all sorts of gadgets and gismos related to daily life there. It gives a surrealistic impression, looking up at the massive Hopewell Centre; it looks like a white solid column accidentally landed in the wrong place and became a landmark. You can tell directions by looking at it from the streets and alleys around. This sort of landmarks should not happen too often, or else they will lose their significance as landmarks. The coexistence of extra-large and extra-small on the same street is precisely a characteristic of Hong Kong Style. The harmony of scales in western theories is not applicable here. High-density urban spaces and short life-cycles of buildings give Hong Kong a collaged cityscape.

華潤大廈是另一種風景。它是典型的香港上世紀八十年代都市規劃的產物，底層是商場店舖，上面是寫字樓，入口的半開放中庭空間感特別強，旁邊都是巨型的高樓大廈。告士打道像一條河，把灣仔新舊區分開了，大大小小的汽車巴士貨車電車像流水一樣，川流不息，華潤則是這條大河的一個標記。相對於附近的中環廣場用上了大量雲石建造的大堂，華潤倒有種平實的作風；相對於三座政府辦公大樓，華潤又多了幾分嚴肅。華潤是灣仔填海新區的第一代大樓，記得以前鷹君中心的新華戲院仍然存在的時候，每次都會穿過告士打道行人天橋，再到華潤，經過中藝百貨公司，再到戲院。華潤擁有香港第一代的架空平台式「街道」，成功之處是比較有空間感，「街道」比較闊，不限於一條單向的窄通道，而是開揚和可以讓人停下來的流動空間。

The CRC Building is another kind of landscape. It is a typical outcome of the urban planning of Hong Kong in the 1980's. On the lower levels are shops and shopping mall, above are offices; the semi-open atrium entrance has a particular strong sense of space, and surrounding it are mega towers. Gloucester Road is like a river separating the old and new parts of Wanchai, with streams of cars, buses, trucks and trams flowing along, and the CRC Building is a marker on the river. In comparison with the marble-clad lobby of Central Plaza nearby, the CRC Building has a non-pretentious way of being, and even becomes more solemn alongside the three government office blocks. The CRC Building belongs to the first-generation towers of the Wanchai reclamation area. I remember when Columbia Classics Cinema in Great Eagle Centre still existed, I would pass through the Gloucester Road footbridge to get to the CRC Building, then would pass by the Chinese Arts and Crafts department store to arrive at the cinema. It is the first generation of elevated platform "streets" in Hong Kong; its success lies in its strong sense of space, with wide "streets" and not some narrow one-way corridors, thus becoming an open and flowing space that allows people to take a stop.

　　最近華潤附近進行大裝修，香港大學專業進修學院也搬到附近，一些中小型的咖啡名店酒吧也相繼出現，新的「社區空間」設於冷氣空間外，處於有風有空氣有陽光的平台上，是閒時喝咖啡讀書、與朋友聊天的好地方。

The area around the CRC Building is recently under major renovation: HKU SPACE has moved in, and various smaller cafés and bars are operating there. This new "community space" is located outside on the platform where there is natural wind and air and sunshine without air-conditioning, making it a good location for having a coffee, reading or chatting with friends in leisure.

　　華潤地面的入口十分「怪雞」有趣，九龍壁和獅子擺設十分後現代。旁邊的所謂中式石屎公園有點怪相，設計師實驗性的用石屎建造中國庭園，不大成功，相信改為單純以樹木為主的公園更佳，也可以讓港灣道多一個戶外的空間和廣場。夏日裡站在華潤高樓底的地面大堂也是一種視覺經驗——室外強烈的陽光與戶內的「幽暗」空間形成強烈的對比。華潤大廈的重頭百貨公司中藝是香港百貨業的老字號，裡頭有很多寶，細心尋覓，自有收穫。現時國貨公司的所謂現代化，磨蝕了舊有國貨公司的特色和性格，變得和其他百貨公司沒有分別。中藝暫比較能夠保持自我，但在無情的全球經濟競爭之下也隱約在變，其實不必。

The entrance of the CRC Building on the ground level is bizarrely interesting, decorated with a post-modern mural of the nine dragons (the origin of the name Kowloon, which literally means 'nine dragons') and stone lion sculptures. The adjacent so-called "Chinese style" garden in concrete looks strange. The architect's experimental attempt to build a Chinese garden in concrete does not seem to be a great success. It could work better if the park is simply themed in greens with trees, and that would also give some outdoor space and a plaza for the neighbourhood of Harbour Road. It is such a visual experience to stand under the tall floor space of the CRC lobby during summer – the bright sunlight from outside is making striking contrast with the dim interior space. The major store in the CRC complex, Chinese Arts and Crafts, is one of the oldest names in the Hong Kong retail industry. There is a lot to discover in the store, and one would find his/her treasure for sure if one looks carefully. Now, the Chinese products emporiums under the so-called "modernisation" reform, have eroded away the originality and personality of old Chinese products stores and have become indistinctive to other department stores. Chinese Arts and Crafts is still holding onto its personality, although it is changing in a subtle way under the heartless pressure of globalisation. Actually, the changes are unnecessary.

中西合璧
»East Meets West«

　　中國的建築物自清朝起已開始引用西方的建築觀念，創造出「折衷主義」的風格。香港作為英國殖民地，一直在繼續做這方面的實驗，但是失敗比成功多。

Chinese architecture has been infused with Western architectural concepts since the Qing dynasty, creating a style of eclecticism. Hong Kong, having been a British colony, has continued to experiment in this aspect, but there are more cases of failure than success.

　　香港常常被稱為一個「中西合璧」的城市。中西合璧可以有很多不同的層面，由意識形態到外表形態、視覺語言。建築學裡有所謂「折衷主義」的風格，可以用來分析和形容這種中西合璧的建築。

Hong Kong is known as a city of "East meeting West". The integration of east and west can be in many different levels, from ideology to exterior form to visual language. In architecture, there is a style called eclecticism to describe this mixture of two architectural styles.

　　這種風格最重要的例子是清朝的圓明園，可惜的是我們現只可以在圖畫和相片裡看到它的面貌。到了民國時期，部分接受西方建築設計訓練的建築師，開始實驗中西合璧，結合西方的建築技術和中國的設計語言。董大酉先生是其中的代表人物，南京的中山堂、上海的同濟中學都是這種中西合璧的實驗作品。

The most important example would be the Yuan Ming Yuen park of the Qing dynasty; unfortunately we can only see it in paintings and photos now. In the early 20th century, some of the western-trained Chinese architects started to experiment with this eclectic style, integrating western architectural technology into the Chinese design language. Mr. Dong Dai You is the most representative figure, Chong San Hall in Nanjing, Tongji Secondary School in Shanghai are products of experimentation in the eastern-western style.

西方結構　中國佈局
Western Structure with Chinese Organisation

香港的殖民歷史背景提供了一個更多元的實驗場所，我們在香港的不同角落都可找到中西合璧的實驗品，由珍寶海鮮舫又金又紅、又龍又鳳的通俗設計、虎豹別墅大屋民間工匠的天堂地獄主題公園設計、大大小小的廟宇，到受明朝古墓設計影響的中銀大廈大堂，用的都是西方工業革命發展出來的石屎和鋼筋水泥結構，但空間佈局和裝飾設計語言則從中國不同地域的設計找靈感。

Its colonial background has given Hong Kong a diverse space for experiments, and we can find different cases of "east meets west" here and there in Hong Kong. From the kitsch design of red and gold dragon and phoenix of the "Jumbo Seafood Boat"; the heaven-and-hell theme park of "Tiger Balm Garden", a mansion of traditional arts and crafts; or temples in various scales; to the atrium of the Bank of China building which was influenced by mausoleum design of the Ming dynasty... All these were constructed with concrete and steel, products of western industrial revolutions. However, in terms of spatial organisation and decoration/design language, they took inspiration from different Chinese regional designs.

香港的建築師斷斷續續在做着這些實驗，沙田的車公廟是近年較為成功的一個例子，建築方法和技術是西方的，但佈局和空間偏向吸收了中國傳統廟宇建築的概念。

Architects in Hong Kong have been doing this kind of experiments intermittently, the Che Kung Temple in Shatin is a successful example using western method and skills, but with a concept of traditional Chinese temple for spatial design.

失敗的例子比成功的多，沙田的文化博物館正正是最失敗的，建築師粗暴地引用四合院概念，眼高手低，整體空間的佈局體積過大，沒有四合院那種流動空間的格局，不符合比例的中國式瓦頂與整體建

像東蓮覺苑這類廟宇，用西方石屎和鋼筋水泥結構，來配合中國傳統的空間佈局和設計語言。*Tung Lin Kok Yuen (a Buddhist nunnery) is a temple using the western structure of concrete and reinforced concrete with traditional Chinese spatial organisation and design language.*

虎豹別墅
Tiger Balm Garden
虎豹別墅是很多三十歲以上香港人的集體記憶。小時候長輩總用裡面的天堂
地獄壁雕教導我們要做好事做好人。年紀大了，明白這些雕塑就是非常特別
的藝術作品，能夠保留下來的話，得益的不單是旅遊業，香港的下一代也可
以認識到香港的傳統。*Tiger Balm Garden is the collective memory of many
Hong Kong people over 30 years old. When I was small, the elders always
used the figures in the heaven and hell wall sculptures in the garden to
teach us to be good. When I became older, I came to understand that
these sculptures are very special works of art. If we could keep these
works, it would benefit the tourism industry, and let the generations to come
know more about the tradition of Hong Kong.*

蓮花宮

Lin Fa Kung (Lotus Temple)

大坑除了有一年一度的舞火龍，也有蓮花宮。蓮花宮的設計十分特別，是典型的「折衷主義」，入口的金魚池、內部兩層空間的設計，與典型的中國廟宇十分不同，左右兩個入口也十分罕見，充滿西方中古時期小型教堂的設計味道。*In Tai Hang, there is the Lotus Temple as well as the annual fire dragon dance. The design of the Lotus Temple is very special, of typical "eclecticism". At the entrance is a gold fish pond; and the double-storey space of the interior is in great contrast to the traditional Chinese temple. The design of two entrances, one on the right and one on the left, is also very rare for Chinese temple. The style of this temple is similar to that of a western church in medieval times.*

珍寶海鮮舫
Jumbo Floating Restaurant
珍寶海鮮舫的大紅大金，十足十的唐人街香港風格。中西合璧之處在於滿足西方對中國的慾望和想像，是屬於拉斯維加斯那種徹底的通俗。王家衛的《花樣年華》其實也是相同的概念，不過對象不是水兵，而是小資產階級知識分子，這種中西合璧屬於無傷大雅的一類，好玩誇張最重要。 *In the design of the Jumbo Floating Restaurant there are a lot of red and gold, very typical of Chinatown and Hong Kong style. The "east meets west" here is to satisfy the fancy and projection of westerners for the Chinese. It is the Las Vegas kind of kitsch. Actually, Wong Kar Wai's movie, "In the Mood for Love" is playing the same game, but its targets are not sailors, but petty-bourgeois intellectuals. This sort of east meets west is rather harmless, and the point is to be over the top and have some fun.*

東蓮覺苑
Tung Lin Kok Yuen
跑馬地賽馬會會所附近、山村道上的東蓮覺苑，是少數擁有完整中西合璧風格的建築物，雖然手法仍然是比較表面的裝飾風格，但其中國風格的裝飾不會像珍寶海鮮舫那樣誇張與通俗，比例和配色十分平實，是非常值得保留的香港傳統建築。廟宇平日局部向公眾開放，參觀時留意大門及大門中間的天窗空間。*The Buddhist nunnery Tung Lin Kok Yuen, located in Shan Kwong Road, Happy Valley near the Jockey Club, is one of the very few buildings in Hong Kong constructed in a concept that is utterly east-meets-west. Though its style might not go beyond its surface of decorative design, its Chinese-style decoration is simple, unlike the tacky and over-the-top embellishment of the Jumbo Floating Restaurant. The proportion and colours of the Buddhist nunnery are plain and simple; and the building should be well preserved as a sample of traditional Hong Kong architecture. Part of the temple is open to the public, and when you go there for a visit, pay attention to the space between the main entrance and the skylight.*

築物並不協調，最失敗的就是非常重視出入口設計與佈局的四合院概念，在沙田博物館卻找不到它的任何影響。

There are more failed examples than successful ones, like the Heritage Museum in Shatin. The architect has brutally applied the concept of Chinese "Siheyuan", courtyard house to the design inappropriately. The Museum's overall spatial volume is over-scaled, thus missing the fluidity in design of a courtyard house, and the out of scale quasi-Chinese style tile roof is not in harmony with the overall structure. The most defeating point is that there is nothing special regarding the design of the entrance, which is one element that courtyard houses emphasise most.

這種偽中國建築風格也是在香港常常出現的一種現象，說明設計者和業主對中國文化、建築的認識不深，以為有斜瓦就是中國建築，甚麼都說是四合院概念。

This fake Chinese architectural style is a phenomenon frequently seen in Hong Kong that shows the designers and property owners have insufficient knowledge in Chinese culture and architecture. They believe when there is an inclined tile roof, it means it is Chinese architecture and anything with that could be considered a "Siheyuan".

志蓮淨苑後現代感覺
Post-modern Impression of Chi Lin Nunnery

中國建築風格非常多元，四合院只是其中一種概念和風格，不同區域發展了不同的特色。香港身處華南地區，與西方和其他文化交流的機會比較多，所以風格也較為多元。只是我們近年習慣了在高樓大廈生活，大部分香港人也不太察覺這些富有特色的建築存在，能夠保留下來的大都是與宗教或教育有關的建築。

Architecture of China has a very diverse style, and the Siheyuan (courtyard house) is only one of them. Different regions have developed different regional characteristics. Hong Kong, being in the South China region, has more opportunities for exchange

近年香港的中西合璧實驗，既有成功也有失敗：沙田車公廟（上）成功地吸收了傳統廟宇的建築概念；而沙田文化博物館（下）套用四合院概念卻顯得生硬膚淺。 *In recent years, there are cases of success as well as cases of failure in the experiments of fusion between oriental and western designs in construction style: Shatin Che Kung Temple (above) -- the architectural concept of traditional temples is successfully implemented here; Hong Kong Heritage Museum in Shatin (below) -- the Siheyuan (courtyard house) concept is inappropriately applied here, making it look a bit forced and superficial.*

with western cultures, therefore the styles here are more diverse. Because we are used to high-rise towers, most people in Hong Kong do not realise the existence of some Chinese architectures here with unique features, and the ones which are preserved are usually religion- or education-related.

　　志蓮淨苑的仿唐設計其實也是一種折衷主義的實驗，任何仿古建築都含有一點想像和重新演繹的色彩。志蓮的重要性是，在香港這種極端功利的情況下，能夠運用一種不符合成本效益、仿古的木建築方法興建，與四周的建築格格不入。從大老山隧道望向荷里活廣場與志蓮淨苑，感覺特別後現代，也是十足的香港風格：充滿矛盾與複雜。The pseudo-Tong Dynasty design of the Chi Lin Nunnery is also an experiment on eclecticism. As any architecture imitating ancient ones, it has a certain amount of imagination and reinterpretation. The importance of the Chi Lin Nunnery is that under the extreme utilitarianism situation in Hong Kong, it was built with a less cost-effective, ancient wood construction and it stands out from the surrounding architectures. Looking at Hollywood Plaza and the Chi Lin Nunnery from the Tate's Cairn Tunnel, it gives a particular post-modern impression which is unquestionably "Hong Kong Style": full of contradictions and complications.

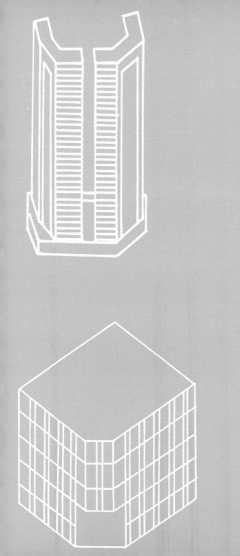

歷史的湮沒與改造
The Annihilation and Transformation of History

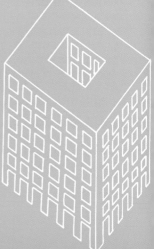

老社區的滅絕
»The Extinction of Old Communities«

　　在過去十多年間，不少香港的老社區都因重建而消失。最近政府發表有關未來舊區重建的諮詢文件，以較理性和長遠的態度看待問題，至於如何具體落實則仍是個謎。

During the last two decades, many old communities in Hong Kong have disappeared for the sake of urban renewal. Recently the government has released a consultation paper seeking views regarding urban renewal, with the hope of handling the issue with a more rational and long-term attitude, although the way of specific implementation is still a mystery.

　　高地價政策對香港都市生態的破壞難以估計，許多珍貴的歷史建築和舊區在短時間內被政府消滅。上環舊區就是一例，市區重建局的前身土地發展公司，把上環一帶本來是香港人的歷史遺產、文化資源、旅遊景點的老商店和建築徹底消滅，像中環中心現址的得雲茶樓、南北行的南貨店、潮州小食大排檔、舊茶餐廳等都消失了。

The high land price policy has caused numerous damages to the urban ecology of Hong Kong, many precious historical buildings and old districts were destroyed by the government in a short period of time. The old neighbourhoods in Sheung Wan are some examples. The Land Development Corporation, predecessor of the Urban Renewal Authority, had completely destroyed the historical heritage, cultural resources, and scenic spots of old stores and architecture in the Sheung Wan region that belongs to the people of Hong Kong. Tak Wan Restaurant, which is currently Central Plaza, the dried seafood grocery store of Nam Pak Hong, dai pai dongs of Chiu Chow snacks, old-style cafes, have all vanished.

深水埗 Sham Shui Po
深水埗是香港製造業的發源地,也是香港電腦科技的搖籃,鴨寮街、高登商場、黃金廣場,以及大大小小的住宅和工業大廈,構成一個具香港風格的典型老社區,並且保留着一些老商店和老式騎樓底民居。*Sham Shui Po is the birthplace of the manufacturing industry, as well as the cradle of computer technology in Hong Kong. Apliu Street, Golden Computer Centre, Golden Computer Arcade, as well as the various shopping malls, residential and industrial buildings of all sizes create a typical old community of Hong Kong style. In this community, some old shops and old-fashioned arcade houses are still standing.*

舊區特色連根拔起
Uprooting Old Town Characteristics

　　現在的市區重建局應徹底改正以前土發公司的錯誤,以香港長遠利益為前提,着重歷史文化社區發展,重新建立或更進一步地發展原有的社區特色,推動不同社區的民間文化。香港政府的舊重建政策最失敗的是,只顧追求短期的財政利益,每個重建項目都是超級高樓大廈大廣場,把原有的社區特色和文化連根拔起。規劃過程中並不重視設計研究和社區歷史文化的研究,鮮會理會大專院校對都市發展、社區歷史的學術意見。政府做事故步自封,只維護大地產商的利益,卻忽視平民百姓中小企業和民間團體的長遠利益。

舊社區的建築、店鋪的特色均有發展價值，更值得重視的是保存原有的社區網絡。Shops and buildings in old communities have their own characteristics and thus are good materials for development. What is more important is the preservation of the existing community networks.

露天街市、街邊小食、大排檔
Open Air Markets, Street Food, Dai Pai Dongs
露天街市是香港舊區的必需品。主題式的露天街市、露天小食、大排檔是多
年來由民間總結的成果。需要改善的是水電和衛生設備等基本建設支援。
Open air markets are one of the essentials of old districts in Hong Kong.
Over the years, privately-run street stalls have developed into open air
markets with different themes (of goods), street food stalls and dai pai
dongs (open-space cooked food stalls). What needs to be improved is the
basic infrastructure support like running water, electricity and sanitation
facilities.

中港安居置業
TEL: 3486 8655

廟宇 *Temples*
每個香港舊區都必然有廟宇，卻常常遭人忽視。廟宇可以被看作公共藝術、公共空間、香港歷史文化的遺產；像灣仔舊區皇后大道東的天后廟、大坑的蓮花宮，都是香港旅遊業的秘密武器。*Every district should have its own temples, but this is often being overlooked. Temples could be seen as public art, public spaces, and historical and cultural heritage of Hong Kong. For example, Tin Hau Temple on Queen's Road East in Wanchai and Lin Fa Kung (Lotus Temple) in Tai Hang are all secret weapons of Hong Kong tourism.*

The current Urban Renewal Authority should correct the mistakes of the former Land Development Corporation. They should see the long-term benefit of Hong Kong as the prerequisite, and put emphasis on the development of historical and cultural communities, to re-establish or further develop the characteristics of existing communities, and promote different civic cultures of the communities.The biggest failure of the urban renewal policy of the Hong Kong government is the singular focus on short-term financial profit. Every renewal project is building super tall towers and extra large plazas, uprooting the original community characteristics and culture. During the planning process, little importance is placed on design research and cultural studies; and very rarely attention is given to academic advice from institutions regarding urban development and community history. The government is being too conservative, with policies favouring the profits of large property developers, and neglecting the long-term benefits of the common people, middle and small enterprises and NGO's.

規劃環境地政局發表的有關舊區重建的諮詢文件，能以較理性和長遠的態度看待舊區重建問題；保存具歷史、文化和建築等價值的樓宇、地點及建築物，保存地方特色和區內居民的社區網絡等，都被列入重建工作的目標。

Our government could treat the old town redevelopment issue with a more rational and long-range perspective in the consultation paper issued by the Housing, Planning and Lands Bureau. They should include preservation of buildings and places with historical, cultural and architectural values, and also local characteristics and community network on the list of objectives in their redevelopment work.

但如何具體落實這些目標？市區重建局剛剛成立，運作模式透明度低，而且在龐大的財政壓力之下，能否真的落實以上目標，也是一個謎。

How could they realise these objectives specifically? The Urban Renewal Authority has just been established and their operation model has a very low level of transparency. Furthermore, under huge financial pressure, it is still a mystery whether the above objectives could be realised.

請政府浪子回頭
Urging the Government to Change

若根據昔日土發公司的方案，要重建灣仔舊區，就要把所有舊區建築完全消滅，區內非常具歷史和建築價值的建築物，例如灣仔舊街市，將被銅鑼灣時代廣場式的大型發展取而代之，所有的舊社區的特色和網絡就此失傳，絕對是香港的悲劇。

Should the previous proposal of Lands Corp for rebuilding the old town of Wanchai follow through, they would destroy all old buildings in the area. Local buildings with great historical and architectural

騎樓底建築 *Arcade Architecture (Storey Over Sidewalk)*
騎樓底是典型亞洲風格的建築,也是香港老建築特色之一,好處是夏天不怕太陽曬,是很環保的設計。上海街、灣仔仍保留一些擁有這種設計的樓房。這種設計應該在香港未來的新建築物大量使用。*Arcade houses are typical of Asian style architecture, and are also one of the old architectural characteristics of Hong Kong. Arcade architecture is a very environmentally friendly design, and it provides shade from the sun. In Wanchai and Shanghai Street (Yaumatei), there still remain some arcade houses with covered sidewalks. This design should be largely used in future for Hong Kong's new buildings.*

在銅鑼灣的舊區加入時代廣場這種大型發展，顯得格格不入。*It is so out of place to put large development projects, like The Times Square, in the old district of Causeway Bay.*

時代廣場：香港港島銅鑼灣勿地臣街1號
Times Square Hong Kong: 1 Matheson Street, Causeway Bay, Hong Kong Island

values, such as the Wanchai Market, would be replaced by large development project in the style of Times Square in Causeway Bay. All the special features and network of the old neighbourhood would be lost thereafter, and it would certainly be a tragedy for Hong Kong.

　　經過百多年發展出來的香港特色、香港風格，在這短短十數年，就被政府一手消滅。這說法好像有點偏激，但卻十分真實。現在政府浪子回頭，唯一可以寄望的就是能夠把仍然存在的舊區，好好的重建和發展下去。

The government has, in a dozen of years, single-handedly destroyed the Hong Kong characteristics and style developed through a hundred years. This statement might sound a bit radical, yet it is very true. The government should put a stop to that, and our only hope is that we could preserve the existing old districts and redevelop them in a decent manner.

鄉郊風味哪裡去了？
»Whatever Happened to Our Countryside?«

　　香港人口都是高度集中在幾個區，鄉郊的面積其實很大，很多大大小小的村落散佈在鄉郊裡。大部分傳統村落都是華南地區的圍村，遵循中式「四合院」的規劃，建築設計上富有華南民居建築中西合璧的特色。

The population of Hong Kong is concentrated in several zones in the city. The area of the countryside is actually very large, with many big and small villages scattered around. Most of the traditional villages are walled-villages of the Southern China region, built following the structure of Chinese "Siheyuan" (Chinese quadrangles, which literally means a courtyard surrounded by four buildings), with the East-West cross-cultural style of Southern Chinese residential architecture.

　　清末民初時期的香港鄉郊村落以中國式建築為主，元朗新田大夫第就是很好的例子。所謂傳統圍村，是以城牆一樣的圍牆包圍着由不同大小庭園組成的大型四合院。可是重修後的大夫第，沒有了人氣，好像失去了一種靈氣。

Country villages in Hong Kong during the early 20th century were mostly built in Chinese architectural style, the Tai Fu Tai Mansion in San Tin, Yuen Long is a good example. The so-called "walled-village" is a large scale Siheyuan composed with different courtyards and surrounded by a wall. Unfortunately, the Tai Fu Tai Mansion after renovation seems to miss a human touch and its spirit is lost.

　　我總覺得中國建築和西方建築最大的分別是在於「人的位置」。西方建築強調以建築宣揚神的偉大、人的渺小；中國建築則強調建築空間和人的關係，以人為本，所以中國建築喜歡向橫平面地發展，西

大天第這條傳統圍村，雖有幸得以保存舊貌，但周圍的規劃全不配合，破壞無遺絕倫的構圖；而重修後的大天第，也失去了人氣。 Tai Fu Tai Mansion is a traditional walled village built in the reign of the Qing Dynasty. Though its appearance of ancient dwellings is preserved, the surrounding architectural planning does not integrate into the whole picture, and now the composition looks absolutely absurd. After renovation, the Mansion seems to have lost its spirit and a human touch.

本來充滿中國華南傳統鄉郊風貌的新界，今日的景觀有如「四不像」，假如在二十年前離開，今天沒有可能認出這就是本來富有農村風味的新界。這是誰的錯呢？ *The New Territories used to be very rustic, filled with traditional rural characteristics of the South China region. Now, its landscape is nondescript, lacking distinctive qualities. If you had been away for 20 years, you wouldn't have recognised this to be the New Territories, which used to be so idyllic. Whose fault is it then?*

方則是向上發展。

In my opinion, the greatest difference between Chinese and Western architectures is on the "position of man". Western architecture stresses on the greatness of architecture versus the smallness of humans, while Chinese architecture focuses on the relationship between space and man, with the emphasis lying on man. Therefore, Chinese architecture is usually in horizontal development, while western ones are skywards.

傳統的中國民居建築的思維，功能和空間的關係不是絕對的，陽光、空氣和水的元素很重要，可惜這種以人為本的建築已經不再，今日的鄉郊，很難再找到這種建築。就算有，也可能沒有人居住。現在流行的是所謂西班牙式的「村屋」，二至三層高的。

In the concept of traditional Chinese residences, there is not an absolute relationship between function and space. Light, air and water are also important elements. It is such a pity that this sort of human-based architecture does not exist anymore. It is difficult to find this type of architecture in the countryside today; even if there are some, they are probably abandoned. What is popular right now are the so-called Spanish-style two to three-storey "cottages".

上世紀五、六十年代的村屋十分有研究價值，特色是結合傳統與現實——樓底高，通風好，方方正正的直線橫線，用料是當時流行的「洗水米」，顏色美麗。最有趣的是這些小屋的屋頂都刻有落成的年份，1958、1962、1960等等的數目字，成為建築的一部分，房子變成了一個歷史符號，一個有機體，十足意大利建築師Aldo Rossi的作品。

The village house from the 50's and 60's is worth studying. Its characteristic is the integration of tradition and reality – tall floor height, good air circulation, square and formal lines, with the then-popular "washed beige" as material, beautifully coloured. An interesting note about the village house is that the year of completion is engraved below the roof in the front entrance: 1958, 1962, 1960 … the number became part of the architecture, the house became a historical signifier, an organic element, just as the works of the Italian architect, Aldo Rossi.

早年的村屋，建築以中國農村小屋為基礎，我們的新界村屋還有個特色，就是有建造年份，堂堂皇皇的成為建築設計的一部分。 *The early village houses were built with references to China's rural cottages. The village houses in the New Territories share the same attributes, with the year of completion as part of the architectural design.*

　　上世紀七、八十年代開始興起的「西班牙式」設計，大都是三層高的，用瓦磚砌成所謂「西班牙式」的斜面屋頂。這種所謂「西班牙式」別墅村屋當然不可能在西班牙找到，可能只是文化想像的產物，但這種設計已完全破壞了香港鄉郊村落的面貌。

The "Spanish style" design became popular during the 70's and 80's; most of the buildings are three-storey high, with a so-called "Spanish" inclined tiled roof. Certainly this sort of "Spanish style" architecture cannot be found in Spain, and is a cultural product of Hong Kong mentality only. Yet this sort of design has totally destroyed the face of the countryside in Hong Kong.

　　香港政府的鄉郊規劃也是完全失敗的，由於丁屋政策，政府不負責任地把鄉郊的規劃以「太公分豬肉」的方式處理，把村屋並排地建在一起，屋貼屋，門對門，窗對窗，以前圍村的四合院格局以及鄉郊的大自然環境完全沒有納入在規劃之內。

現在的新界，遍佈在西班牙永不會找到的「西班牙式」別墅村屋，這種
完全不顧及自然環境的設計，大煞新界的風景。 *Now, all over the New
Territories, there are numerous "Spanish villas", which could not be found
in Spain. This kind of "Spanish style" architecture, with total disregard for
the natural environment, is really an eye-sore and ruining the landscape of
the New Territories.*

Rural planning by the Hong Kong government is also a total failure. Due to the Small House Policy [1], the government has irresponsibly planned the rural area with a so-called "fair share" treatment. It results in villas packed in rows, wall to wall, door across door, without the slightest consideration for the human factor of the previous Siheyuan style, or the natural countryside atmosphere. These important human factors were not considered at all during planning.

香港的鄉郊很多富有傳統風味的村落，已被「西班牙村」破壞，大煞風景。香港的文化遺產並沒有受到應有的衝擊，西貢和大嶼山還好，上水、元朗、大埔一帶是重災區。露天貨櫃場的出現，更令鄉郊的大自然風味盡失，香港政府要承擔全部的過失，所謂重視傳統只是嚷嚷的口號，實質的工作完全沒有做！

The "Spanish villas" have left an unbearable sight that damages many villages rich of traditional flavour. The cultural heritage in Hong Kong did not receive the right kind of stimulation. The situation in areas such as Sai Kung and Lantau Island is not that bad, but Shun Shui, Yuen Long and Tai Po are badly hit. The sight of open-air cargo storage spaces makes the countryside stripped of its natural colours, and the government of Hong Kong is to be blame for this disaster. What they say about "valuing traditions" is only a slogan, and no practical work is done!

---

1. Small House Policy (丁屋政策): A policy established in the 70's by the British government to allow each indigenous male villager to build one small house in villages in the New Territories.

Reinvent 尖東
»Reinventing Tsim Sha Tsui East«

尖東現在給人的印象，是過時、落後的二流商業購物區，是聲色犬馬江湖人物的休閒娛樂場所，是邊緣少年流連的避難所……但這些印象正好反映了尖東的親民和多元，也反映了尖東的潛力。潛力就匿藏在各幢中等高度建築物，以及建築物之間的廣場和行人專用區之中。

Tsim Sha Tsui East (TST East) gives an impression of being an outdated, second-rate commercial/shopping area with entertainment venues for gangsters, a hide-out for marginal youth…yet, this reflects accordingly the "down-to-earth" and diverse nature of TST East, and also the potential of the area. The potential lies in the clusters of mid-rise buildings, and the plaza/pedestrian zones among them.

尖沙咀東部是香港城市規劃的特別個案，因為該區是高地價政策實施之前最後一個格子系統 （grid system） 設計。高地價政策實施以後，香港政府的都市規劃中，以前街道為主的格子系統，轉變為堡壘式的中央巨型系統，像沙田新城市廣場、太古廣場，在一個巨型平台上面坐落了多幢高層大廈。這種中央集權式的管理概念和規劃概念不容許社區（community）的形式，不容許任何不符合中央大業主規管的活動，個人和小團體小商戶遂被大集團利益取代。

TST East is a special case in the urban planning of Hong Kong, since it is the last grid system design prior to the high land price policy. Ever since the execution of the high land price policy, urban planning in Hong Kong has transformed from a grid system with the streets as focus into a castle-like gigantic centralised system, like the New Town Plaza of Shatin or Pacific Place, with a number of towers built on top of a large podium. This type of centralised management and planning concept does not allow the formation

尖東是香港最後一個作格子系統設計的社區，現在看來極具特色。 *Tsim Sha Tsui East is the last community in the urban planning of Hong Kong to have a grid system design. It now appears very unique.*

尖東有可能成為世界上景色最壯觀的海邊廣場。*Tsim Sha Tsui East could have been the harbour side plaza that possesses the most magnificent view of the world.*

of communities; it does not allow any activities not complying with the rules of the management. Individuals, small groups and small businesses are replaced by profiteers of large corporations.

露天茶座和街頭表演
Open-air Cafés and Street Performance

尖東的 grid system 組合了多幢中等高度建築物。建築物之間有多個廣場和行人專用區，成為公共空間，讓市民參與和交流。廣場旁邊的建築物可以發展各種各樣的露天茶座、大排檔、流動小販、街頭表演，成為具有香港特色的市集、市民的活動中心。

The grid system of TST East consists of many mid-rise buildings, and among them are many plazas and pedestrian zones, which are public spaces that encourage participation and interaction of people. The plazas could be developed into spaces for all sorts of open-air cafes, dai pai dongs, street vendors and street performances. It can become a bazaar with Hong Kong characteristics, an activity centre for the public.

尖東現在需要的是公共用途的重整，以及具體設施的重新設計。用途重整包括：容許廣場和行人專用區的商舖發展露天茶座、容許各式各樣的街頭表演、義賣活動。具體設施的重新設計包括：戶外照明、大廣場的街道家具（street furniture）、植物或園景（landscape design）設計，以及連接海濱公園和九龍車站的天橋。

What we need in TST East right now is a reorganisation of public spaces, and a redesign of facilities. The reorganisation of functions for the spaces includes: allowing the shops in the plazas and pedestrian zones to develop into open-air cafés, allowing different sorts of street performances and activities of charity vendors. The redesign of facilities includes: outdoors lighting, street furniture for the plazas, landscape design, and a bridge connecting the harbour-front park with Kowloon Station.

華懋戲院 *Chinachem Cinema*

華懋戲院是香港唯一接近24小時營業的戲院，在上世紀八十年代末、九十年代初的香港電影高峰期，晚晚都人山人海，各路英雄、平民百姓都在這裡找尋娛樂。附近的車仔麵店也是尖沙嘴夜市中最好吃的，價錢又相宜。*Chinachem Cinema is the only cinema in Hong Kong that operates overnight. In the late 1980's and the early 1990's, during the peak of the Hong Kong film industry, the cinema was crowded with people from all walks of life every night. It was a hot spot of entertainment for the common people. The cart-noodle shop nearby serves the best food among all similar eateries in Tsim Sha Tsui during the night, and at a very low price too.*

尖東很多店鋪仍停留在上世紀七、八十年代做遊客生意的格局。*Many shops in TST East still remain in the 70's and 80's, lacking personality, catering mainly for tourists.*

最壯觀景色的海邊廣場
The Magnificent Harbour-side Plaza

尖東規劃最失敗的地方是以一條路把該地區和海濱公園隔起來，若這條大路改為設在地底，讓公園和尖東連結起來，便可以成為香港海邊廣場了，這將會是擁有世界上最壯觀景色的廣場！

The worst part of the TST East planning is the road that separates the harbour side park from the rest of the area. If this road could be made underground so TST East and the park could be connected, then it would become the harbour side plaza of Hong Kong that possesses the most magnificent view of the world!

尖東的大廈商場其實可以重新定位，發展主題式商場，像針對年輕人的時裝流行文化產品、書城、影音產品等等香港小型商戶組合。

The identities of the TST East shopping malls could be re-defined, and the malls could be redeveloped into themed shopping centres, targeting young people and their interests, like fashion and cultural products, books and audio-visual gadgets. It would be like a combination of units of Hong Kong small businesses.

現在尖東的商場缺乏性格，很多仍然停留在上世紀七、八十年代做遊客生意的形象。租金已下調，尖東有空間開發一些新形式的零售業務。香港的活力不是來自大企業，而是千千萬萬的中小型企業和個體戶，尖東正好重新發展為一個民間文化、娛樂和飲食的商業區。

The shopping centres in TST East currently lack personality, many of them still remain in the 70's and 80's, catering for tourists. Rent has been reduced and there is space to develop some innovative types of retail services. The energy of Hong Kong does not come from large corporations, but thousands of small and medium enterprises and individual businesses. It is the perfect time for TST East to redevelop itself into a commercial area with folk culture, entertainment and restaurants.

華懋廣場戲院：香港九龍尖沙咀麼地道77號
Chinachem Cinema: 77 Mody Road, Tsim Sha Tsui East, Kowloon, Hong Kong

由廣場組成的公共空間，是尖東的特色之一。 *The public spaces among the many plazas are one of the characteristics of TST East.*

老尖遊記
»Travelogue on "Lo Tsim"«

　　尖沙咀彌敦道一帶至海旁叫作「老尖」，這個舊區一直沒有受人注視，其實值得細心研究，從中可以發現一些早已失落的建築設計價值與傳統。
We call the part of Tsim Sha Tsui (TST) along Nathan Road to the harbour "Lo Tsim" (Old Tsim). Not much attention is paid to this old district, yet it is a place worth studying in detail. Here, one can find some lost traditions, values and architectural designs.

　　尖沙咀是香港舊區中最重要的「遊客區」，以前的西方遊客大多喜歡在尖沙咀購物。洋服、鐘錶、首飾、電器、相機、工藝品、「行貨畫」，都可以在尖沙咀大大小小的商場和店舖找到。
Tsim Sha Tsui is the most important "tourist area" among the old districts of Hong Kong. In the past, most visitors went shopping in TST. In the various shopping malls and stores in TST, one can find custom-made clothes, watches, jewellery, home appliances, cameras, handicraft works and mass-produced paintings .

　　重慶大廈因為王家衛的電影《重慶森林》而世界聞名，其實旁邊的美麗都大廈在建築設計上比重慶大廈更有特色，也是尖沙咀中小型店舖的後援基地，有洋服店工場、首飾和鐘錶修理工業、行貨油畫室、小型加工以及各式各樣、令你意想不到的小店……沒有美麗都大廈，尖沙咀的旅遊零售業就失去了重要的支援。
Chungking Mansions became world-famous because of Wong Kar Wai's movie "Chungking Express", although the adjacent Mirador Building actually has more character in its architecture and design. Mirador Building is also the base of support for many medium/small shops of TST. In the building, there are tailor workshops, jewelry and clocksmith ateliers, mass production arts workshops, small post-production factories and all kinds of novelty shops... Without Mirador

美麗都大廈 *Mirador Mansion*

Building, the retail sector of TST would lose an important backup.

　　最近路過尖沙咀，想起往日在東英大廈的經驗，舊地重遊，發覺沒有現在典型暴發戶式的雲石水晶燈裝修，樓上辦公室面向九龍公園的景色仍然十分優美。旁邊的美麗華酒店也是尖沙咀的老房子，近年進行了大整容，卻是俗氣的雲石空間，更令我覺得東英大廈的可貴。

Passing by Tsim Sha Tsui recently, I thought of my former experience with Tung Ying Building in the old days. Now revisiting the place, I could not find any typical parvenu style of marble and crystal chandelier here, and the view of Kowloon Park from the offices is still very pleasant. The adjacent Miramar Hotel is also an old establishment of Tsim Sha Tsui, it went under major reconstruction

美麗都大廈: 香港九龍尖沙咀彌敦道54-64 號B
Mirador Mansion: 54-64B Nathan Road, Tsim Sha Tsui, Kowloon, Hong Kong

美景都大廈內部都是小商鋪、小工場，是尖沙嘴零售業支援基地。In Mirador Building, there are small shops, ateliers and workshops, and they serve as a base of support for the retail sector of Tsim Sha Tsui.

尖沙咀街坊會旁的教堂，見證了香港殖民地歷史的轉變。*The church next to the Tsim Sha Tsui District Kaifong Welfare Association has witnessed the transformation of Hong Kong's colonial history.*

聖安德烈堂：香港九龍彌敦道138號
St. Andrew's Church: 138 Nathan Road, Kowloon,
Hong Kong

recently, and unfortunately it has become a vulgar space of marble. This has made me realise how precious Tung Ying Building is.

　　香港其實也有一些像東英大廈一樣建於上世紀五、六十年代的現代主義高樓，非常值得保留，其設計的經典水平足以成為香港的文化遺產，也是香港人集體記憶的一部分。東英大廈採用的高樓大廈設計語言是很好的教材，包括：現代主義物料應用的法則、中國文字幾何圖像與西方現代建築的「結合」、街道比例與建築高樓大小之關係等。

There are other modern buildings in Hong Kong from the 50's and 60's like Tung Ying Building that deserve preservation. Their classic designs should be regarded as cultural heritage of Hong Kong. They are also part of the collective memory of Hong Kong people. The design language applied to Tung Ying Building is exemplary, such as the rule of Modernist application of materials, the "integration" of Chinese geometric characters with western modern architecture, and the relationship of the scale between the street and building height.

　　普通人看東英大廈是主觀經驗多過理性分析，現在東英大廈商場內店舖比較呆板老化，若裡面有多一些具特色的店舖咖啡室，會是個好地方。上世紀五、六十年代的香港大廈都很會用「中文字」，曾經見過一幢住宅用的都是全黑的石，上面有一欄也安裝了中文大廈的名稱「承業大廈」，也是黑色的，十分前衛。(按：東英大廈於2006年被拆卸。)

For a layman, looking at Tung Ying Building is more a subjective experience rather than a rational analysis. Now, shops at Tung Ying Building are rather stale and old-fashioned. Should there be more shops and cafes with distinguishing features, the building would become a great place. In the last century during the 50's and 60's, buildings in Hong Kong made good use of "Chinese characters". For example there is a residential building in black masonry throughout, with the Chinese name "Shing Yip Building" installed on the facade, also in black, very avant-garde. (Note: Tung Ying Building was demolished in 2006.)

　　彌敦道尖沙咀段是香港樹氣最旺的大道，兩旁的古樹比台北仁愛路的樹還要高要大。可惜過了倫敦戲院之後的彌敦道就沒有任何大樹了。特別珍惜尖沙咀彌敦道的大樹，前身是尖沙咀街坊福利會的古物古蹟辦事處，見證了尖沙咀的轉變，殖民地西方加中國的建築設計，旁邊的教堂，後面的天文台，像走進時光隧道的老香港，四周圍的樹特別多特別高，對比九龍公園的設計，這些樹木對香港來得更有意義。尖沙咀幾個老公園改建以後都沒有「老」的感覺，像覺士道公園和九龍公園，人工味過重，已經不像公園了，樹木花草和人分得太清楚，像露天商場而不是公園。

The Tsim Sha Tsui part of Nathan Road is the most prolific tree-lined boulevard in Hong Kong; there are ancient trees taller and bigger than those in Jen-ai Road of Taipei. Unfortunately there are not any large trees on Nathan Road from London Cinema onwards. The large trees in Nathan Road of TST are particularly precious. The Antiquities and Monument Office, the former TST Neighborhood Association, has witnessed the transformation of the area. It is in western colonial architectural style plus Chinese design, with a church next door and an observatory behind. Being there is like walking into a time tunnel and seeing the old Hong Kong. Trees in the surrounding area are particularly tall and abundant; they are more meaningful to Hong Kong in comparison with the design of Kowloon Park. Several old parks in TST have lost the "aged" atmosphere after renovation, such as the Cox's Road Park and Kowloon Park. They are too artificial and do not look like a park anymore. They seem like open-air shopping mall where man and nature are set too much apart.

　　尖沙咀沒有太多的露天茶座，酒吧卻不少。那兒的酒吧和中環銅鑼灣的很不一樣，十分「草根」和「地道」。就算是遊客，到酒吧也一樣招呼，沒有中環的中產味。柯士甸道、金巴利道、金馬倫道、河內道組成的酒吧區，大大小小各適其適，遊客在這裡可以知道很多關於這個城市的故事。酒吧內播的音樂、雞尾酒的調製水準、主持人的待客之道、酒客談論的話題、酒吧的空間設計……觀察這些事物，也是一種有趣的體驗。

There are not too many open-air cafés in Tsim Sha Tsui, yet there are quite a few pubs and bars. Pubs here are quite different from

those in Central or Causeway Bay; here they are very "grass-root" and "local". Service is the same for locals and tourists, without the middle-class atmosphere as in Central. Austin Road, Kimberly Road, Cameron Road and Hanoi Road form the pub-zone, with various establishments catering to different tastes. Visitors can learn many stories about the city here. The music played in these bars, the quality of the cocktails, the service by the hosts, the issues discussed by the customers, and the spatial design of the bars... observing all these can be an interesting experience.

香港文化中心
»Hong Kong Cultural Centre«

　　位於九龍尖沙咀的香港文化中心、太空館和藝術館，是非常好的建築設計反面教材——由整體佈局、建築形態、功能設施，以及物料運用，都完全違背了建築設計的原則。這些違背，不是故意搞創新，而是不折不扣的九流設計。

The Hong Kong Cultural Centre, Space Museum and Hong Kong Museum of Art situated in Tsim Sha Tsui, Kowloon are good materials to give negative examples of architectural design – from the overall organisations, architectural forms, facilities and functions to the use of materials – they all go against the principles of architectural design. These violations of principles are not intentions for breakthrough, but simply bad designs.

　　九流設計由粉紅色的「物料」開始，整座文化中心及其範圍，由地面到牆上，都鋪滿粉紅色的磚塊。地方形磚的日常打理十分浪費資源，工序繁複，卻始終似是衛生條件不佳的小廁所。當然整個文化中心的設計概念就是一座超巨型的低級公廁：沒有窗，沒有空間。戶外的空間佈局也是怪彆扭的：廣場不似廣場，不三不四的，枉費了維多利亞港的景色；四周種了毫無生氣的椰樹；長方形的水池是典型的外行設計；鐘樓與環境格格不入，十分怪相。

We can talk about the horrible design of Hong Kong Cultural Centre by starting from the pink "materials". The whole complex of the Cultural Centre, from floor to wall, is covered with pink tiles. Those square tiles on the ground are difficult to take care of, and it is a waste of resources for their maintenance. They make the place look

香港文化中心, 香港太空館, 香港藝術館：香港九龍尖沙咀梳士巴利道10號
Hong Kong Cultural Centre, Hong Kong Space Museum, Hong Kong Museum of Art: 10 Salisbury Road, Tsim Sha Tsui, Kowloon, Hong Kong

香港文化中心　*Hong Kong Cultural Centre*
香港太空館　*Hong Kong Space Museum*
香港藝術館　*Hong Kong Museum of Art*

like a toilet in poor hygiene condition. For certain, the design concept of the whole Cultural Centre is a gigantic third-rate public toilet, without windows, without any sense of space. The organisation of outdoor space is also weird and twisted: the plaza does not look like a plaza, with spiritless coconut trees planted around. In fact, it does not look like anything, wasting the great view of Victoria Harbour. The rectangular fountain is typically a non-professional design; and the clock tower does not integrate well with the surrounding environment, and looks extremely odd there.

文化中心的外形大而無當，美感欠奉；內部大堂的空間佈局，欠缺重心和清晰比例，條形天窗小家子氣十足，望向港島的香港會議展覽中心，其入口大堂起碼符合基本建築設計的空間天線比例要求。

The shape of the Cultural Centre is large yet impractical, without any sense of beauty; the interior spatial organisation lacks focus and clear proportion. The linear skylights are petty, looking towards the Convention Centre in Hong Kong Island. At least, the design of the entrance atrium of the Convention Centre complies to the basic requirement of proportion of architectural space to the skyline.

不客氣的說，文化中心設計之差劣，簡直是香港這個國際城市的一個污點。當務之急是馬上着手研究文化中心的「重建設計」。這裡說的重建不是把整座建築物拆了再建一座新的，而是把戶外的空間重新佈局，把空間的用途具體化，加強與維多利亞港的互動。文化中心外牆的物料當然要改，增加透明的空間，重新分配內部大堂的功能，調撥更多空間用作茶座或咖啡座。

Frankly speaking, the horrible design of the Cultural Centre is indeed a stain of Hong Kong, the international city. It is most urgent that we should start considering and studying "rebuilding" Cultural Centre. "Rebuilding" here does not mean demolishing the building and replacing it with a new one, but reorganising the outdoor spaces, making the functions of these spaces more practical, strengthening the interaction with Victoria Harbour. For sure, they have to change the materials for the exterior of the Cultural Centre, increase transparency in the interior spaces, reallocate functions of spaces in the lobby, and allocate more space for bars and cafés.

飯盒
»Lunch Box«

　　香港人每天消耗數以百萬計的飯盒。飯盒的設計，看來簡單，其實反映着一個地方的環保文化和價值觀。飯盒就是「食物包裝」，上世紀八十年代以前，香港的食物包裝以「紙」為主要材料，經典的當然是白紙配雞皮紙袋，街頭的小吃，如豬腸粉、串燒、魚蛋⋯⋯都是用這種經典的包裝系統，再高檔一點就是硬皮紙設計。紙是有機物料，用來包裝食物，感覺上既健康又環保。在美學和觀感上，紙製的食物包裝或者飯盒，樸素平實，體現了簡約主義的精神。

People in Hong Kong consume millions of food container every day. The design of a food container or a lunch box seems to be plain, yet it reflects the environmental culture and value of a place. The food container is essentially "food packaging". Prior to the 80's, most food packaging in Hong Kong used paper as material; and white oil paper with a kraftpaper bag is a classic, for street snacks such as steamed rice-rolls, barbecue skewers, fish-balls... all were packed in this classic way. Packaging in cardboard was a grade more superior. Paper is an organic material, to use it for food packaging seems healthy and environmentally friendly. In terms of looks and aesthetics, paper bags and paper containers for food packaging is honest and plain, and manifests a minimalist spirit.

　　塑膠材料出現後，紙包裝逐漸被取代。八十年代以後香港的食物包裝完全是塑膠物料的天下，飯盒都是以發泡膠為主。發泡膠飯盒的設計主要分為兩大類——一件過的蓋連身，以及蓋和身分開的——顏色都是白色，蓋面通常印上紅色的食店標記。茶餐廳、茶樓、酒家、快餐店，都用這種發泡膠飯盒取代了昔日以紙為主要材料的傳統。

Since the invention of plastic and styrofoam, paper packaging was gradually replaced. Ever since the 80's food packaging is dominated by plastic materials, most food containers are made of styrofoam. Styrofoam containers can be divided mainly into two categories,

one uniformed box with cover, and the other kind with two separate pieces - the colour is always white, usually with the restaurant logo in red. All cafes, restaurants, fast food shops use these styrofoam boxes to replace traditional paper containers.

　　紙符合環保原則，因為可以自我分解，發泡膠則需要極長時間才能分解。從設計的角度來説，紙飯盒設計的可塑性高，容許不同食店發揮自己的風格，像中環的鏞記酒家，依然保留紙飯盒的傳統。茶餐廳未大為流行以前，香港的廉價飯盒主要由快餐店供應，這些飯盒也是紙製的，紙製飯盒的缺點是容易滲漏，但只要花一些心思，問題是可以解決的。

Paper is good for the environment because it is biodegradable, whereas styrofoam takes an extremely long time to dissolve. From a design point of view, paper food container has high malleability that allows individual restaurants to express their style, for example, Yung Kee Restaurant in Central still maintains the tradition of using paper containers. Before "Cha Chan Teng" (Hong Kong style cafes or tea restaurants) became widely popular, economical lunch boxes were provided mainly by fast food restaurants, and the containers were made of paper. Food containers made of paper have a problem of leakage since they are not waterproof. However, the issue can be solved if we put in more thoughts.

可惜在香港這個急功近利和注重短期效益的城市，超廉價的發泡膠飯盒自然成為主流。日本的環保便當膠飯盒在香港也不流行，原因也是成本兩個字。而香港各大型連鎖式快餐店也是用發泡膠飯盒，因而對生態環境造成極大的破壞。到將軍澳垃圾堆填區看看，就會發現香港每天製造的垃圾是何其多，當中就有數以百萬計的發泡膠飯盒！台灣去年立法禁止使用發泡膠飯盒，十分正確。但香港的環保政策總停留在「得個講字」的層次，要實施垃圾分類較登陸月球更困難，因為香港目前的垃圾處理流程，被官僚系統主導，而官僚系統往往缺乏想像力和改革原動力。像發泡膠這個現象，是必須由政府提出立法才能改善的。

Unfortunately, in Hong Kong, a city of quick money and instant benefit, styrofoam lunch boxes at super low cost have naturally become the mainstream. The eco-friendly bento boxes popular in Japan do not work in Hong Kong either, for the same reason of "cost". All large fast-food chains in Hong Kong use styrofoam containers, and this creates great damages to the environment. Take a look at the Tseung Kun O landfill, then one will realise the quantity of rubbish produced by Hong Kong every day, and there are millions of styrofoam boxes there! A few years ago, there was a ban on using styrofoam boxes in Taiwan, and that was a correct move. However, the environmental protection policy in Hong Kong stalls at the level of "empty talks". It is probably more difficult to land on the moon than to implement waste division, because the process of waste treatment in Hong Kong is overruled by bureaucracy without imagination and motivation to reform. In fact, to stop this phenomenon of styrofoam containers, it is necessary for our government to introduce a policy and do something.

可喜的是民間這幾年也有一些食店主動以較環保的材料作為飯盒之用，翠華茶餐廳就是一例。也有一些小食店開始使用環保型的飯盒，設計上更美觀，也更環保。發泡膠飯盒實在十分可怖，尤其是載入高溫食物後，便會出現一種「倒模」現象，若是雞翼便會在盒內壓出雞翼的profile，不用說，吃進肚子的雞翼必然帶有「發泡膠物質」，對身體一定沒有好處，但大部分香港人天天都在使用這種不良飯盒！飯盒的設計應該是有很多可能性的，健康和環保才應該是飯盒設計的基本原則，物料應該是可以自我分解的有機體，紙是最好的材料。現在更有一些具環保概念的新塑膠材料，容許發揮設計創意的可能性是更多。

Yet it is nice to see there are some eateries in town using some environmentally friendly materials for their food containers, and the Tsui Wah chain is one of them. There are also some smaller restaurants using green containers, more pleasing to the eyes in design and more environmentally friendly. Styrofoam food containers are actually quite horrible, for there will be a "molding" effect when containing high-temperature food. For example, with hot fried wings, the profile of a chicken-wing will be impressed onto the box. Needless to say some part of the styrofoam will go into our stomach with the chicken wing. This would certainly do no good to the body, yet most people in Hong Kong are using these terrible lunch boxes everyday! There should be great possibility in the design of food containers. Health and eco-friendliness should be the basic principles of their design, and their materials should be organic and self-degradable. Thus, paper should be the best choice. There are some eco-friendly plastic materials invented recently, allowing even more possibilities for creativity.

香港作為一個「國際大都會」，在環保這個主題上應該走得更前、更快，但發泡膠盒這個現象，説明香港的環保意識仍然屬於發展中地區的階段，既離奇又不合理。作為經常享用飯盒的香港人，應該以消費手段鼓勵更多具環保意識的食店。

Being a metropolitan, Hong Kong should take a leading role in this issue of environmental concern. However, the phenomenon of styrofoam boxes indicates that the ecological consciousness in Hong Kong still remains on the plain of a developing country. It is quite absurd and unbelievable. Being citizens of Hong Kong, who consume lunch boxes frequently, we should encourage eco-friendly eateries by way of consumer's choice.

大廈的名字 · 樓盤的姓氏
»The Name of the Residence«

　　中國人很重視姓名，相信名字和命運有着不可分離的關係。近十年來，香港樓盤的命名呈現一個特別現象，就是喜歡用「豪」「帝」這兩個字，如海逸豪園、帝景園、麗豪閣，總之就是豪 × 園、× 豪園、× × 豪庭、帝 × 閣、× 帝園……又帝又豪背後就是一種暴發戶的價值觀吧？就好像要全世界都知道所住的地方又豪又帝。「海」和「天」是比較流行的另行兩個字：擎天半島、海 × 園……天和海屬大自然，比較平實，但大部分香港的高樓都看不見天和海，這類名字或許能給住客一種對天和海的幻想。

The Chinese attach great importance to names, and believe that names and fate are closely linked together. Over the last decade there is a curious phenomenon on the names of real estate and property. There is a particular interest in using the word "grand" and "majestic". Isn't it the value of the nouveau riche behind the repeated words of "majestic" and "grand"? It's just like you want to tell the whole world your residence is so grand and so majestic. The other two words that are also commonly used are "ocean" and "sky": "Ocean" and "sky" belong to nature, they are rather simple and regular, and however, most of the buildings in Hong Kong do not have views of the sky and ocean. Perhaps, this sort of names would give the residents an illusion of nature.

　　名字對單幢大廈和由幾十幢大廈組成的大型樓盤自然有不同的功能。跑馬地的單幢大廈很着重自己的身份，例如景光大廈就是在景光街上的，而尖沙咀山林道就有松林大廈，大廈的名稱和街道的名稱經常都有關連。尖沙咀柯士甸道的正記大樓是老大廈，是單純的住宅大廈，樓下是幾十年的老店「雲裳」，賣造衣服的材料。

There are different functions in the name for a single building and that for a property composed of many towers. The stand-alone buildings in Happy Valley have strong identities, for example "King

愉景灣是最受外籍專業人士歡迎的屋苑之一，但這兒從屋苑名稱、樓宇建築到環境規劃，都是最簡樸實用的設計。Back to Basic 是世界大趨勢，只有香港炒樓文化繼續沉醉於置發戶的意識形態。 *Discovery Bay is one of the most popular residential estates among the foreign professionals in Hong Kong. Here, everything is of the simplest and most practical design, from the names of the buildings, the architecture, to the environmental planning. Back to basic is the trend of the world now; and only the property speculation culture in Hong Kong is still indulging in the ideology of the nouveau riche.*

Kwong Building" is located on King Kwong Street, and there is the "Pine Tree Building" on Hillwood Road in Tsim Sha Tsui. The names of the buildings are usually related to the names of the streets. The Tseng Bros Buildings on Austin Road in Tsim Sha Tsui is an old structure, a simple residential building, with a decades-old fabric shop "Wen Shang" (meaning "cloud dress" literally).

　　樓宇的名字是一種記憶符號，舊式的香港樓宇名字比較容易記起，如彩虹邨、坪石邨、愛民邨、太古城、沙田第一城、美孚新邨、愉景灣、黃埔花園、玫瑰新邨等，都簡單直接。新樓盤的名稱很平庸，難以留下印象，YOHO Town 是近年比較有意思的，行銷策劃也在玩這八個英文字母，馬上把它從其他同類型樓盤區分開來；其廣告重點是「生活」品位，而不是超豪會所、雲石大堂。相比之下，同期推出的藍澄灣就缺乏性格，若改名為藍天花園就會突出一點。

The name of a building is a symbol of memory. The older properties in Hong Kong have names that are easier to remember, such as Choi Hung (Rainbow) Estate, Oi Man (Love People) Estate, Taikoo Shing (Swire Town), First Town Shatin, Mei Foo Sun Chuen (Mobil New Estate), Discovery Bay, Whampo Garden, Rose Garden, etc... they are all straight-forward and direct. The newer properties have indistinctive names that are difficult to leave an impression. YOHO Town is one that is more creative, also the marketing strategy of this property is playing on the eight letters of YOHO Town, one can distinguish it from the other properties at once. Their advertising focus is on "lifestyle" and not luxurious clubhouse or marble lobby. In comparison, Rambler Crest on sale at that same time lacks personality; it might be more outstanding if it is named Blue Sky Garden after the Chinese name which has "blue" in it.

　　香港人花費大部分的收入在居住方面，但對設計的要求卻不太講究，重視的是交通是否方便以及是否擁有一些和空間質素無關的材料，有些時候單是名字，便能決定一個樓盤的命運。香港在上世紀九十年代，越來越少單幢樓宇的發展概念，大部分都是多幢式的大型發展，在樓盤的名稱也越來越不着重特色。

People in Hong Kong spend a high proportion of their income on their residence, but not many of them care about the design of the building. What is important is traffic convenience and expensive materials that have nothing to do with the quality of space. Sometimes, the name of the building alone would decide the fate and prosperity of the property. In the 90's, there was less and less development of standalone buildings, and the market went for multi-tower large complexes. Also, less and less care was given to the names of projects.

　　泡沫地產時期，樓盤一推出便自然有買家了；1997年後地產泡沫破滅，樓市不再是炒家市場，而是用家市場，發展商有必要調整其規劃概念和設計模式。規劃上應着重社區的身份特徵，與社群的互動，愉景灣便是成功的例子。

During the bubbling period of real estate, there would be buyers lining up once a real estate project was out in the market. Since the burst of the real estate bubble in 1997, the property market became a market not for speculators but for users, and there was a need for property developers to adjust its planning concept and design method.

　　設計上應在空間質素多下工夫，如樓底的高度，露台的配置以及空間的格局，不應浪費金錢在建設雲石大堂和不切實際的會所。住在「街道的環境」，比較有人氣，大型樓盤的設計到處一樣，令人不辨方向，裡面的大廈的名稱也經常令人摸不着頭腦。

There should be more emphasis on the community and identity during planning, and also more interaction with the residents, and Discovery Bay is a successful example. In terms of design, there should be more thoughts on spatial quality, such as floor height, placement of balcony and spatial organisation. Money shouldn't be wasted on building marble lobbies and luxurious clubhouses. When living in a "street like environment", there would be a better sense of humanity. The plans and designs of large properties are identical and confusing, and one is unable to make any sense of the names of the buildings.

政府美學的謬誤與批判
The Fallacies and Critiques of Our Government's Aesthetics

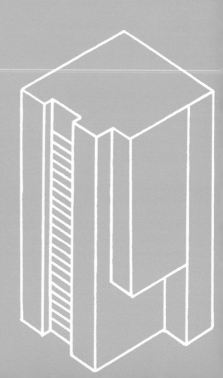

監獄主義
»Prison-ism«

香港的公共建築設計，絕大部分由建築署包辦，建築署設計的主流是一種監獄式的風格。這種風格在上世紀八十年代初期形成，任何建築計劃落在建築署手上，他們都有本事建出一座監獄來，在外面包到密密實實，方便官僚的控制。

The Architectural Service Department (ASD) does most of the designs for public structures in Hong Kong, and the majority of their works follows a style of "prison-ism". This style was formed during the 1980's, and whenever a project goes into their hand, the ASD would build a prison out of it. The structures are all enclosed and airtight from inside out, for the convenience of bureaucratic control.

學校被高高的圍牆包圍，教室就像牢房，每間學校都一樣；安老中心也築起高高的圍牆，老人居住在四面是牆、監獄一樣的房間；大街小巷裡被高高鐵欄包圍着的小公園鋪滿了石屎，長椅也被金屬扶手截成一格格的迷你監獄。新近建成的政府辦公大樓是公務員的監獄：樓底低、沒有天然光、中央冷氣、雲石大堂。法院的設計也活像監獄一樣，比較一下終審法院和新建成的法院就明白。

Schools are surrounded by high walls; classrooms are structured like prison cells, and it is the same in every school. Elderly homes are also surrounded by high fences, and the elders live in rooms that are enclosed and prison-like. Neighbourhood parks are fenced and built in concrete; even the benches are fragmented into mini-cells by iron armrests. The newly built government office complex is a prison for civil servants: with low ceiling height and no natural light, but only central air conditioning and marble lobby. Even the courthouse is like a prison, it is obvious should one compare the newly built courthouse with the old Court of Final Appeal in Central.

政府總部給鐵枝封起來後，下亞厘畢道也失去了流動空間的感覺。*After the building of the Central Government Offices was enclosed by iron bars, the previous feeling of flowing space in Lower Albert Road is lost.*

灣仔政府綜合大樓 (灣仔政府大樓，入境事物大樓，稅務大樓)
The Government Towers in Gloucester Road (Wanchai Tower, Immigration Tower, Revenue Tower)

灣仔政府大樓: 香港港島灣仔港灣道12號
Wanchai Tower: 12 Harbour Road, Wan Chai North, Hong Kong Island
入境事物大樓: 香港港島灣仔告士打道7號
Immigration Tower: 7 Gloucester Road, Wan Chai, Hong Kong Island
稅務大樓: 香港港島灣仔告士打道5號
Revenue Tower: 5 Gloucester Road, Wan Chai, Hong Kong Island

告士打道政府大樓
The Government Towers in Gloucester Road, Wanchai
這個由三座超級大廈組成的建築群，設計的時候究竟有沒有經過深思？辦
公室樓底低，在裏面工作的公務員肯定不好受。入境事務大樓人多的時候
空氣更差最奇差，內部燈光也過分強烈，簡直是「白色恐佈」。 What were
they thinking when they built this architectural complex of three high rise
towers? In the offices, the ceiling is low and civil servants working there
are definitely having a hard time. Air ventilation is particularly poor in
Immigration Tower. The internal lighting is too strong, and it is like working
under "white terror".

密密麻麻、一排排的政府辦公室，就像公務員的監獄。Government offices are tightly packed on both sides of the corridor. It is like a prison for civil servants.

從學校、安老中心，到皇后大道中這個小公園，工務局建築署甚喜歡用鐵欄圍起來。 The Architectural Services Department likes to use iron railings to enclose all things, from schools to nursing homes, to this small park in Queen's Road Central.

建築文化水平低
Low Standards in Architectural Culture

　　建築設計反映業主的文化水平和能力，香港政府的建築文化水平
是比低還要低。是香港政府管治無力？是建築署無能？公務員的整體
水平有問題？還是公共工程的決策過程出現了問題？

Architectural design reflects the property owner's cultural standard
and ability; and the standard of the Hong Kong government
in architectural design is lower than "low". Is that a failure in
management of the Hong Kong government? Is it the inability of the
Architecture Department? Or is it a problem of the overall standard
of civil servants in general? Or is it a problem of public works policy?

　　香港的政府建築在八十年代以前奉行平實的現代主義。美利大廈
的窗口設計是環保建築的示範單位。中環大會堂的低、高座和中庭是
香港最具代表性的現代建築，內部的音樂廳和劇院設計，從聲音反射
設計到整體的格局，都是香港最有氣派的表演場地。九龍醫院的石
屎旋轉樓梯入口，是一件具有實際功能的雕塑作品。中環政府總部西
翼的黑色入口隆重莊嚴，西北兩翼之間建有的廣場，但回歸之後，政
府用鐵枝把它包圍起來，以前下亞厘畢道的流動空間感覺也失去了。

Before the 80's, government architecture in Hong Kong advocated
simple and honest modernism. The window detail of the Murray
Building is an exemplary work of eco-architecture. The lower and
upper blocks of City Hall in Central, along with its courtyard, are
most representational of modern architecture in Hong Kong: the
interior designs of its Concert Hall and Theatre are classics of Hong
Kong's performing arts venues, from their acoustic systems to overall
organisations. The circular staircase at the entrance of the Kowloon
Hospital is a functional sculpture. The west wing of the Government
Secretariat in Central has a solemn entrance in black, with a plaza
between it and the north wing. However, after the handover in 1997,
the plaza was enclosed with iron bars, and the previous atmosphere
of flowing space at lower Albert Road is lost.

皇后大道東的小公園
The Small Park in Queen's Road East.

小小的一個公園，竟然動用大量鐵閘圍困著，坐在裡面就像坐牢，或像困在動物園裡的鐵籠。誰有心情在那裡休息？好好的一片空地，為甚麼不可以讓市民自由自在地享受，讓他們多一點人邊乘涼，遠看天賣月。*It is only a small park, but it is enclosed by a large number of iron gates. One would feel like being imprisoned, or an encaged animal in a zoo, sitting in this park. Who would enjoy a sense of leisure there? This is a nice open space. Why can't they let people enjoy it freely? Grow some trees here, and people could rest in the shade and watch the moon.*

九龍醫院的旋轉樓梯，既是雕塑，也具實際功能。*The spiral staircase in Kowloon Hospital serves both as a sculpture and practical function.*

官僚紙上談兵
Armchair Strategists and Bureaucrats

香港政府的公共建築政策並不是由懂建築的建築師主導，遊戲規則都是由官僚紙上談兵地規劃出來，欠缺對人的關懷，沒有視野和理想。公共建築直接影響一個城市的形象、當地市民的歸屬感，香港欠缺的，正正是讓香港人感到自豪的公共建築。

The government policies of public architecture in Hong Kong are not made by professional architects who know about architecture. Regulations are drawn by bureaucrats, by way of "idle theorising", that does not care for humanity, and is without vision and any sense of mission. Public architecture affects directly the image of a city and the sense of belonging of its people. What is missing in Hong Kong is public architecture that our citizens can be proud of.

監獄主義建築反映了香港政府自我封閉和井底之蛙的心態。政府常常說設計很主觀，沒有好或不好。多麼無知和反智！設計是學問、是專業，監獄主義設計就是反智的證明！

"Prison-ism" architecture reflects the self-enclosed and myopic (frog-in-the-well) mentality of the Hong Kong government. The government always says that design is very subjective and there is no "good" or "bad" per say. What an ignorant and anti-intelligence comment! Design is skill and knowledge, a profession. Design in ways of prison-ism is anti-intelligence!

設計也是 common sense，一種生活的態度；設計從功能出發，但最終目的不是處理功能，而是人類的心靈。香港政府的監獄建築把香港人的心靈牢牢的封閉起來，是香港的不幸。

Design is also common sense, an attitude of life. Design stems from function, but its ultimate goal is not just to be functional but to answer the needs of our soul. It is such a misfortune for Hong Kong to have a government that builds prisons to confine the soul of its people.

居住機器
»Machines for Living«

　　香港大約有一半人口居住在公共房屋。公共屋邨設計的演變就是香港平民百姓的生活歷史。早期公共屋邨的設計風格都是現代主義的樣本，重視的是通風和社區空間的多元性。

About half of Hong Kong's population lives in public housing estates. The development of public housing design is the history of the life of the common people in Hong Kong. The early public housing estates are examples of modernism, and issues such as air circulation and the diversity of community spaces were regarded with high importance when they were built.

　　石硤尾「H」型屋邨是第一代公屋，建築成低，樓高九層的空間比較接近人的比例，「H」型的兩個中庭空間是鄰舍交流的地方，問題是衛生設備不好。後來的公屋有了獨立的廁所和廚房，代表作包括背山的蘇屋邨、面海的華富邨、彩虹邨、北角邨等。

The "H" type housing estate in Shek Kip Mei is the first generation of public housing. It was built in low cost, with 9 stories, something closer to human scale, and two community courtyards in an "H" shaped plan. The problem of these housing projects was poor sanitary conditions. Later came estates with better facilities like individual bathrooms and kitchens, and exemplary works include So Uk Estate by the hillside, Wah Fu Estate facing the sea, Choi Hung Estate, and North Point Estate.

現代主義信徒
Disciples of Modernism

　　蘇屋邨説明了樹是建築的靈魂，身處在充滿樹的空間，心情自然開朗。樹下有老人家在乘涼、小孩在遊玩，正好表現這種公共空間的功能。

So Uk Estate illustrates that trees are the soul of architecture. Being around greens would make a person more cheerful. Under the shade of trees there are elders resting and children playing, manifesting the function of this sort of public space.

經已消失的北角邨是香港最值得保存的公共房屋建築，小露台、建築物之間的中庭、大樹、簡潔和低成本的營造設計，是香港的遺產（heritage）。

North Point Estate, which no longer exists, should have been preserved with top priority among all public housing estates in Hong Kong. It had small balconies, courtyards, and large trees among the structures, and it was built with a clean form and low construction costs, and that was supposed to be the heritage of Hong Kong.

現代主義着重實際功能，例如：窗口的大小、窗台的設計、空間的高度和格局、空氣的流通、社區的關係、建造的方法……建築和汽車一樣，是可以大量生產的機器。北角邨的設計明顯受了德國現代主義設計學院包浩斯（Bauhaus）設計哲學的影響，說明建築在工業革命以後作大量生產的可能。現代主義信徒相信，建築師可以設計出一種可以大量生產的居住機器。

Modernism places high importance on practicality, for example: the size of windows, the design of enclaves, the height and organisation of spaces, the relationship of communities, and the method of construction... Architecture is similar to automobiles; they are "machines" that can be mass-produced. The design of North Point Estate was obviously influenced by the philosophy of the German modernist design school of Bauhaus, which shows the possibility of mass production, a concept developed from the industrial revolution. The modernist believes that architects can design living machines built by mass production.

人口密集促使香港成為現代主義的信徒。大坑附近的勵德邨，是香港眾多共屋邨中最具個性和特色的，圓形的空間規劃和外形、內部的圓形中庭、每層樓的公共空間、背山的樹群，沒有雲石大堂，沒有會所，沒有中央冷氣的商場，有的是風、是樹、和空間。

受包浩斯（Bauhaus）設計哲學影響，公共屋邨成了可以大量生產的居住機器。With influence from the design philosophy of the Bauhaus, housing estates turn into living machines built by mass production.

單邊走廊
Single-Loaded Corridor

單邊走廊（single - loaded corridor）是一種通風的設計，在舊式屋邨常常找到，只有一邊是建築物，另一邊就是戶外空間，開了門，空氣自然會流通得好。這是很簡單的設計，但高地價政策之下，這種設計已經在香港絕跡。 *Single-loaded corridor is a design with good ventilation, and it can be easily found in old housing estates. Flats are built on one side and outdoor space on the other side. With the door open, air circulation in the house is good. This is a very simple design, but under the high land price policy, this design is completely wiped out in Hong Kong.*

中庭
Atrium

多條單邊走廊包圍起來就是一個中庭。「H」型屋邨就是兩個中庭，中庭的好處是天氣熱時好乘涼，鄰居也可以在下面互動，中秋節賞月，打麻將、小朋友嬉戲，種種社區活動都可以出現。中庭裏面種一棵樹，長大之後就是一種記憶的符號。 *With several single-loaded corridors around, an atrium is formed. There are two such community courtyards in the H type housing estates. Atriums are good as cool resting places during hot weather, and neighbours can have all sorts of interactive activities there. They can gather to watch the moon in Mid-Autumn Festival, or play mahjong, and kids could play all sorts of games there. If they plant a tree in the courtyard, it would become a symbol of memories when it grows tall.*

High population density has made Hong Kong a disciple of modernism. Lei Tak Tsuen near Tai Hang has the most colourful personality among the many public housing estates in Hong Kong. It has a circular plan and form, with a round internal atrium; there are public spaces on every level, and trees along the hillside at the back. There, one would not find any marble-lined lobby, luxury clubhouse, or shopping mall with central air-conditioning. What it has is air, trees and space.

像監獄不像房屋
More Like a Prison than a House

香港人追求的理想生活空間其實十分「平面」，新近落成的公共房屋和私人屋苑大都強調方便！方便！方便！對於空間的要求不太講究，這是高地價政策的惡果。政府本來可以透過公共房屋的設計，建立好的樣板。但行政主導下的官僚房屋政策重視的是建屋的速度、管理的方便，而不是生活空間的開拓。所以近十年來的公共房屋像監獄多過民居，密密麻麻的面對面地排在一起，沒有樹，沒有風，沒有空間。

The ideal living space pursued by the people of Hong Kong is actually very "two-dimensional". In the newly built public or private housing, all they emphasise is "Convenience! Convenience! Convenience!" One does not ask for much in terms of spatial quality, and that is the adverse effect from the high land price policy. The government could have established good examples through public housing design, but under the executive-led bureaucratic housing policy in Hong Kong, what matters is construction speed and management convenience, and not quality living space. Public housing built in the last ten years feels more like prisons than homes, with towers tightly packed – without trees, without air, without space.

像將軍澳、天水圍這些新市鎮的設計，完全沒有人和社區的概念，居民被當成物件而不是人。這些稱為「和諧式」的公共房屋是現代主義的反面教材，製造方法是倒模的大量生產，但設計的重點不是大量生產出來的空間，而是官僚和政客的數字遊戲。

坪石邨
Ping Shek Estate
彩虹和坪石是在觀塘未開發以前就已落成的屋邨。坪石的特色是一個平台廣場，下面是停車場，上面的平台是一個廣場。廣場四周是不同的商鋪、茶樓、圖書館等社區設施。 *Choi Hung and Ping Shek are housing estates built before Kwun Tong was developed. The special feature of Ping Shek is the podium. The podium itself is a plaza, and underneath it is a parking lot. Around the plaza are shops, restaurants, a library and various community facilities.*

彩虹邨
Choi Hung Estate
彩虹邨是以﹝街道﹞作規劃概念的屋邨設計，一條入口大道，兩旁是茶樓商店。道路的分支是邨內不同的住宅樓宇，中間會有不同大小的廣闊空間。
Choi Hung Estate was built with the design of "streets" being the planning concept. The entrance is one big road, with shops and restaurants on both sides. Residential buildings are standing on the branches of the road, with open spaces of various sizes among them.

中庭作圓形設計的勵德邨，在眾多屋邨中別具特色。 *The circular design of the atrium in Lai Tak Tsuen is very unique among the many housing estates in Hong Kong.*

The design of new towns such as Tseung Kwan O and Tin Shui Wai has totally ignored the concept of man and community, and residents are treated as objects and not people. These so-called "harmonious" public housing blocks are adverse examples of modernism; they were indeed fabricated and mass-produced. However, their design concept was not about mass-production but a game of numbers for the bureaucrats and politicians.

房屋是人類存在的容器，現代主義的精神是人道主義，不是官僚主義，也不是市場經濟。在觀察香港這些舊屋邨建築之際，可以醒覺到一種社區生活正在慢慢消失，當然這種生活理應繼續在香港不同的公共屋邨出現，而不是成為歷史。

A house is a container of man. The spirit of modernism is one about humanity and not bureaucracy, or market economy. Observing the architecture of these older estates in Hong Kong, one realises community life is slowly fading away. This sort of lifestyle of the old estates has all the reasons to remain in the public housing in Hong Kong. It should not become history.

北角邨
»North Point Estate«

　　早前路經北角渣華道，看見舊北角邨已被竹棚重重包圍，相信再過不久，北角邨將會完全消失。這是十分可惜的。(按：北角邨於2004年被拆卸。)

Passing by Java Road in North Point earlier, I saw that the old North Point Estate was covered by bamboo scaffolds. I believed then the Estate would disappear soon. That is a great pity. (Note: North Point Estate was demolished in 2004.)

　　香港島東區的北角邨是香港公共房屋的典範，建築設計和整體佈置是現代主義包浩斯（Bauhaus）式的經典設計，是人道主義的設計，通風設計加陽光，沒有花巧多餘的裝飾，從功能出發。建築之間設有小廣場，居住單位附加小露台，北角邨的設計促進了一種社區的形成，鄰里的出現，這種設計在新型公共房屋再找不到。我反對拆卸北角邨，可惜香港人中「地產經濟」的毒太深，沉迷追求短期的暴利，這種心態令香港難以轉型為多元知識經濟社會，走出當前的經濟谷底。

North Point Estate lying on Hong Kong Island East is an exemplary model of public housing in Hong Kong. Its architectural design and overall layout are classic Modernist Bauhaus designs, with humanistic principles – the designs for sunlight and ventilation are pure and simple, function oriented, without any fancy frills. There are small plazas between the blocks, and a balcony is attached to each residential unit. This design of North Point Estate enhances the formation of a community and reinforces neighbourly feelings, and is something that cannot be found in new public housing estates. I am against the demolition of North Point Estate, but unfortunately people in Hong Kong believe in real estate economy too much, and are obsessed with the pursuit of short-term profits. Having this kind of attitude makes it very difficult for Hong Kong to get out of

北角邨 *North Point Estate*

the current economic downturn and become a diverse society with knowledge-based economy.

　　北角邨是香港建築設計史上非常重要的一頁。九龍區石硤尾的「H」型設計是最早期的公屋模式，當時香港經濟未曾起飛，又有大量新移民從國內湧入，政府遂以最低廉的價錢，興建大批「H」型屋邨，雖然是功能主義主導，但仍能有效凝聚社區，滿足生活的最低需求。單位內有獨立的洗手間、廚房和露台，足令小康家庭安居。

North Point Estate occupies a very vital position in the history of Hong Kong's architectural design. Shek Kip Mei Estate, with its blocks built in "H" shape, is the first public housing estate in Hong Kong. It was originally constructed to alleviate the housing need created by the large influx of migrants from the mainland at that time. The economy in Hong Kong had not taken off yet, and the government built this estate with blocks in an "H" configuration at a low price. Though these blocks were built purely for a functional purpose to meet the minimum requirements of the residents' daily life, they also created a cohesion effect for the community. When Shek Kip Mei Estate was redeveloped later, units were converted into self-contained ones with balconies, private kitchens and toilets, improving the living condition of the residents.

昔日非常興旺的北角碼頭也是坐落在北角邨旁邊，載客與載車的渡海小輪班次頻密。後來把港島東區與銅鑼灣連接起來的東區走廊落成後，配合兩條海底隧道，渡海小輪的功能漸被取代，北角碼頭最後也沒落了。

The North Point Ferry Pier located next to North Point Estate used to be very busy, with ferries carrying cars and passengers running at a high frequency. After the completion of the Eastern Corridor linking Hong Kong Island East with Causeway Bay and the two cross harbour tunnels, the function of North Point ferries gradually dwindled, and North Point Ferry Pier eventually faded away.

我仍然關心的是北角邨裡面的幾株大樹，會否被好好保留。但預期香港政府傾向以行政方便為理由，把它們消滅，這是香港這個文明社會可悲的地方。

I am still concerned whether the few big trees in North Point Estate would be preserved with care. With the usual practice of the Hong Kong Government, handling things on the grounds of administrative convenience, I expect they would be destroyed. This is something so sad about the civilised society of Hong Kong.

街市大廈無人性、無街味
»Markets with No Sense of Humanity«

　　香港是多用途高層建築的鼻祖，政府在上世紀八十年代開始，把一直以街為主的街市，搬到多用途高層建築街市大廈，裡面除街市，還有辦公室、圖書館、體育場地如籃球場、壁球場、羽毛球場。多用途概念其實十分適合香港高密度的環境，但在細節的設計上，這些多層街市反而成為了一個「黑點」和「建築設計的反面教材」。原因是設計指引落伍，建築署和其他政府部門鮮有考慮設計可如何配合氣候和四周環境。

The tradition of mixed-use multi-levels buildings has a long history in Hong Kong. Since the 80's, the government has moved food markets, which should be on the streets, to high-rise municipal buildings. Besides markets, there are offices, library and sports venues such as basketball, squash and badminton courts located in the same building. The concept of mixed-function is indeed quite suitable for densely populated places like Hong Kong. However, on the level of detail design, these multi-level structures have become "stains" and "negative examples" of design. The reason for this is the outdated design guidelines; the Architectural Service Department and other government offices rarely consider that climate and the surrounding should be incorporated into the design.

　　近年落成的跑馬地黃泥涌市政大廈，在地面的一層完全密封，與四周的街舖和街道格格不入，外牆也是粉紅色的廁所磚內用當外用，完全忽略跑馬地這個老社區的特色。街市部分表面上樓底很高，但店舖細得可憐，像石屎小屋，根本不能滿足小型店舖的合理需要。這些政府街市都給管理得很死板，每一家小店可以賣和不可以賣甚麼，都要經過政府審查。

黃泥涌市政大廈地面完全密封，與四周的街舖和街道格格不入，外牆也是典型的粉紅色，廁所磚內用當外用，完全沒有考慮過跑馬地這個老社區的特色。大廈的街市樓底高，但店舖小到不得了，加上政府把街市管理得很死板，每一家小店可以賣和不可以賣甚麼，都要經過審查。 *The Wong Nai Chung Municipal Service Building in Happy Valley has a totally enclosed ground level, that seems very out-of-place with the surrounding storefronts and streets. Pink toilet tiles are misused for the exterior, neglecting the characteristics of the old neighbourhood of Happy Valley. The floor height of the market in the Building is tall, but the stalls in the market are extremely tiny. On top of that, like all government markets, this one is tightly restricted, and everything has to be inspected and approved by the government, even the types of goods on sale.*

The recently built Wong Nai Chung Municipal Service Building in Happy Valley has a totally enclosed ground level, that seems very out-of-place with the surrounding storefronts and streets. Pink toilet tiles are misused for the exterior, neglecting the characteristics of the old neighbourhood of Happy Valley. There seems to be a tall floor height for the market. However, the stalls inside are miserably tiny like little concrete huts, which cannot satisfy the need of small-scale stores at all. All these government markets are tightly restricted; everything has to be inspected and approved by the government, even the types of goods on sale.

上環市政大廈在功能上的確十分多元化，有劇院、展覽館、演藝團體排練和辦公地方、街市、大排檔和體育設施。但因其結構設計的缺陷，通風系統和內部佈局的互不協調，高樓底變成了一個巨型的假天花空間，導致空間不流通，並成為蛇蟲鼠蟻的棲息之所，總有一股奇怪味歷久不散。其實以上環這幅地的面積，街市毋須完全設於戶內。

The Municipal Service Building in Sheung Wan is indeed very diverse in terms of function, with a theatre, an exhibition hall, rehearsal and office spaces for arts groups, a market, food stalls, and sports facilities. However, due to the defect of its structural design, the air circulation and interior organisation are not in harmony. The tall floor height creats a huge false ceiling, causing a problem of air circulation, and furthermore has become a habitat for bugs and mice, with a weird lingering smell… In fact, provided the floor area of this lot in Sheung Wan, there is no reason for the market to be located indoors.

九龍佐敦的官涌街官涌市政大廈的設計比較成功，沒有誇張的外表，通風效果也較佳。但我始終認為街市是屬於街的，新的多層街市設計仍應保留街的感覺。室內冷氣街市不環保，也令街市失去街坊的味道。

The design of the Kwun Chung Municipal Building in Jordan, Kowloon is more successful. The exterior is not overdone and the air circulation is also better. Anyhow, I still hold the idea that the market

新的市政大樓強調多功能，本來頗適合香港的環境，但在細節的設計上卻很失敗。 *All new municipal services buildings focus on being multi-function, which suits the situation of Hong Kong fine, but the design of details is a disaster.*

belongs to the street, and the newly designed multi-levels markets should maintain the impression of "street market". Indoor markets with air-conditioning are not environmentally friendly, and they lose their sense of neighbourhood.

香港仔南朗山道熟食市場的設計較人性化，能顧及用家的需要——簡單的空間佈局，容許大排檔發展自己的特色。
The Nam Long Shan Road Cooked Food Market has a more human design with consideration for the needs of its users – a simple spatial organisation that allows each cooked food stall (dai pai dong) to develop its own character.

這些街市大廈都面對共同的問題：通風、人流和廢水的處理。長久累積的異味及陽光太少，致令三、四樓以上的舖位無人問津，死城一樣。舖位內的設計亦死板如監獄，失去街市應有的靈活和輕巧。
All these market buildings are facing the same problems: air circulation, pedestrian circulation and the treatment of wastewater. The long accumulated smell and lack of sunlight drive people away from the upper levels and make them seem like a deserted place.

官涌市政大廈，通風做得比其他的好。*The Kwun Chung Municipal Services Building has a better ventilation system than its counterparts.*

官涌市政大廈：香港九龍佐敦寶靈街17號
The Kwun Chung Municipal Services Building:
17 Bowring Street, Jordon, Kowloon, Hong Kong

Also, the design of the stores is like that of a prison's, without a sense of lightness and flexibility that markets should have.

上世紀五、六十年代的香港街市大樓，像中環的中環街市、灣仔皇后大道東的灣仔街市，是現代主義建築設計風格的示範作品，尤其重視空間的功能和通風效果；也不會鋪上現時的新型多層街市常見的不耐用也不耐看的瓷磚，因為牆壁只要在一定時間內重新油髹漆一次，便會煥然一新，較更換瓷磚便宜得多。

Market buildings from the 50's and 60's, such as the Central Market and the Wanchai Market on Queen's Road East, are exemplary works of modernism that emphasise on spatial function and air circulation. They would not be covered with those frequently used tiles on new civil buildings that are neither visually pleasant nor durable. The façade would look new if it is repainted periodically, something much cheaper than replacing façade tiles.

這種以實際功能出發的設計，在香港接近失傳。今日的多層街市的設計全部都是一式一樣，錯了也要重複，不斷地一錯再錯，令人嘆息。

This sort of design originates from function is almost lost in Hong Kong. Nowadays, the designs of all multi-level markets are the same, with a lot of mistakes. They would not change, but would keep on repeating their mistakes. It is such a great shame!

學校
»Schools«

　　學校應該是「地靈人傑」的地方，建築設計就是學校的靈魂。好的學校通常都擁有好的學習空間和建築。英國古老的劍橋大學，美國的哈佛、麻省理工、柏克萊，中國的北京大學等「名牌大學」，都是地靈人傑的。香港中學名校的校舍在建築設計和整體規劃上，都很有特色和性格。可惜近年由香港政府設計和興建的學校都遵從監獄式的設計模式，只能反映政府對教育的封閉思想和重質不重量的態度。

A school should be an inspiring and enlightening place that produces outstanding people, and the school's architectural design is its spirit. Good schools usually have good learning spaces and good architecture. Famous universities, such as Cambridge University in England; Harvard, MIT and Berkeley in the USA; and Peking University in China, are all remarkable places with outstanding men. Campuses of renowned secondary schools in Hong Kong have distinguished architectural designs and overall organisations. Unfortunately, in these years the Hong Kong government designs and builds schools following a prison-like prototype, which reflects the government's close-minded attitude on education and its preference for quantity over quality.

　　香港的名校建築設計有幾個特色。首先是校舍的面積比較大，戶外空間也比較多，由低層建築物組成校舍，課室寬敞而且陽光充裕，學生不愁沒有足夠的活動空間。

The renowned schools in Hong Kong share a few common architectural characteristics. First of all, the campus area is usually larger and with more outdoor spaces; the school complex is composed of a cluster of low-rise buildings. Classrooms are spacious and bright, and there are adequate spaces for student activities.

　　九龍華仁中學建於上世紀五十年代，是典型的現代主義設計風格，重視陽光、通風和功能，不搞多餘的裝飾。透光的方式、校舍的佈局，有板有眼。樓底高，有球場、有草地，是合理的學校設計。

Wah Yan College in Kowloon was built in the 1950's, in a typical modernist style that attaches importance to light, air circulation and function, without excessive ornamentation. Illumination and the overall planning of the campus are also orderly and systematically done. It is a reasonable school design with tall ceiling height, a football field and lawn.

　　香港政府慣以香港地少人多為理由，學校校舍都建成高層建築；又把全港學校的設計劃一，以符合經濟原則云云。於是學校就變成「高層監獄」，四處都是牆和鐵閘，戶外空間很少，周圍都鋪上石屎，沒有草地，沒有樹，樓底低，通風效果差，走廊通道窄。這些不似學校的學校，是不懂教育和設計水平低劣的官僚建築師的傑作。香港教育官僚之霸道橫行，可見一斑。若要有效地進行教育改革，應該由改革校舍設計做起。

The government likes to use the excuse of Hong Kong's high population and limited land to build tall structures in campuses. They also standardise all school designs to conform to the principles of economics. Therefore, schools have become "high-rise prisons", with walls and gates on four sides and very little outdoor spaces. It is concrete everywhere, with no lawn, no trees, low floor height, poor air circulation, and narrow corridors. These schools do not look like schools, they are "masterpieces" by third-rate bureaucrat architects who know nothing about education. From this, we can see how tyrannical the bureaucrats are over our education system. If there should be an education reform, it should start with reforming our campus design.

　　拔萃男書院的校舍設計是最佳的榜樣。那是典型英式學校格局，大片的草地和球場，充滿歷史感的主樓，「庭院式」的建築佈局；學習空間不限於課室、戶外草地、大樹下，甚至鼓勵學生在校舍的走廊進行學習或其他活動。體育空間當然重要，但政府建的學校，就是欠缺合格的體育空間。喇沙中學的運動場和游泳池、聖士提反中學的草

香港學校的建築費是台灣的三倍，中國大陸的二十倍，卻擁有最差的通風效果．Construction costs of schools in Hong Kong are three-times higher than those in Taiwan, and twenty-times of those in China, and yet campuses here have the worst ventilation systems

地球場，其實都是學校的必需品。

Diocesan Boys' School has the best of campus design. It is a classic British campus organisation - large lawn and football field, a main building with historical significance, and "courtyard style" architecture. Learning spaces are not confined to the classrooms, and could be in the outdoor lawn, or under the trees. The school even encourages students to have discussions or activities in the corridors. Recreational space is of high importance, but schools built by the government lack decent spaces for recreation. Facilities such as the sports ground and swimming pool of La Salle Secondary School, or the football field of St. Stephen's College are in fact basic facilities of any school.

當然有人會指這些「必需品」不符合經濟原則，但若知道這些「高層監獄」的建造費是如何的高昂，看法必定會不同。香港學校的建造費是台灣的三倍，是中國大陸的二十倍，但設計水平低劣，因為政府沒有建立公開公平的制度來選擇建築設計方案。

Certainly, some would say that these "basic facilities" are not economically effective; however, they surely would not think so should they realise the sky-high construction cost of those "high-rise prisons". Construction costs of schools in Hong Kong are three-times higher than those in Taiwan, and twenty-times of those in China, and yet the designs are so poor. This is all due to the lack of an open and fair system of selection for design proposals by the government.

舊日的學校建築由辦學者主導，與建築師合作愉快，建成的校舍自然忠實反映辦學者的品味和教學理念。像窩打老道的瑪利諾修院學校的校舍，體現教會辦學的「尊嚴」和對人文精神的尊重：不同大小的建築物構成了一個充滿「人情味」的樂園。「人情味」來自空間與人的比例配合，以及室內空間樓底的高度與流動空間的佈局，至於草地和樹木就建構了學生與大自然接觸的靈性空間。

In the past, the building of schools was conducted by people who ran the schools, they had a pleasant working relationship with the architects. Therefore the campuses built honestly and naturally reflected the tastes and education philosophy of the people who ran the schools. For example, the campus of Maryknoll Convent School on Waterloo Road embodies the "dignity" of running a school and the respect for humanity: it is a paradise with "humanity" constructed by buildings large and small. This sense of "humanity" comes from the proper proportion of space and man, along with the spacious floor height and flowing space. Furthermore, the grass and trees create a spiritual space for students to be in touch with nature.

香港的官式學校就是缺乏靈性空間。教育根本屬於靈性的鍛煉，修煉追求知識的方法和態度。靈性空間不能言傳，要親身體會，坐在香港大學陸佑堂的庭院讀一會兒書，自然能夠領會。如有機會在九龍華仁書院的教堂內、拔萃書院的草地上或是香港中文大學舊圖書館停留一會，都能立即感受到官式學校建築所缺乏的優質閱讀空間。

Government-run schools in Hong Kong are in lack of spiritual space. The basis of education is the training of the soul, finding the right method and attitude in the pursuit of knowledge. Spiritual space cannot be described by words, but has to be experienced in person. One could get a glimpse of it by spending some time reading in the courtyard at Loke Yew Hall of the University of Hong Kong. Should one have the chance to stop by for a moment at the chapel of Kowloon Wah Yan College, the lawn of Diocesan School or the old library of Chinese University of Hong Kong, one would be able to feel what quality reading space is, something missing in the schools built by the government.

建築是一門學問，美與不美固然是個人喜好，但美仍是有一套本身的法則，多體驗多學習自然能理解建築功能和美學之間的關係。香港的官員和大部分的官方建築師，都不懂建築，議員又多是井底之蛙，同樣不尊重專家的意見，剛愎自用。最令人難過的是，他們完全沒有自知之明，一錯再錯，不僅浪費公帑，也浪費了讓有才能的建築師發揮的機會，糟蹋了寶貴的學習空間，誤人子弟，實在罪過。

Architecture is a science, whether a thing is beautiful is subjective, yet there is still a set of rules in aesthetics. With more experience and learning one could naturally understand the relationship between architectural function and aesthetics. Most of the bureaucrats and official architects do not understand architecture, council members are like frogs in the well, very stubborn and do not respect the opinions of experts. What is most regrettable is that they do not know their own limitations and make the same mistakes over and over again. This is not only a waste of public money, but also a waste of opportunities for nurturing talented architects. It's a sin to spoil precious learning spaces, misguide students and waste their time.

拔萃男書院：香港九龍旺角亞皆老街131號
Diocesan Boys' School: 131 Argyle Street, Mong Kok, Kowloon, Hong Kong

國際學校
»International Schools«

　　教育政策在這幾年出現了翻天覆地的變化，日日新鮮，但學童與老師每日的活動場所——學校，設計卻一成不變，依然以方便監視管理為出發點，設計一幢幢監獄式校舍，成為香港建築一大特色。

Education policies in Hong Kong have undergone great changes in recent years, and something new comes up almost every day; but the design for schools, the venues for activities of students and teachers, remains the same, focusing on management by monitoring. Our schools are designed like prison houses, and this has become a major characteristic of Hong Kong architecture.

　　看着港大建築系劉秀成教授設計的國際學校校舍，開揚活潑，心裡總不是味兒，難道是金錢作惡，導致出現監獄與樂園的二元對立？非也，歸根究底，一手摧毀學校設計創意的，是無處不在、全球最大的築師樓——香港特別行政區建築署。

It tastes like sour grapes, looking at the open and lively design of an international school by Prof. Patrick Lau, Head of the Department of Architecture of the University of Hong Kong. Why is there the polarity of prison and paradise? Is it just a matter of money? No, the root of all evil is the Architectural Services Department of the HKSAR, which is omnipresent, and has single-handedly destroyed all creativity in school design.

　　劉秀成教授是香港非常少數可以用作者論述分析的建築師，其作品風格是與香港氣候、都市空間和社會文化互動的產物，是名副其實的香港風格。其實在上世紀七十年代以前的香港建築設計，都經常會考慮氣候、環境和城市空間與建築之間的關係，所以住宅大都設有露台或阻隔陽光的簷篷，辦公室的窗戶都設有隔陽光的設計，樓底也比較高，學校的設計也着重綠化和空間的氣氛和感覺。

Prof. Patrick Lau is one of the very few auteur architects in Hong Kong, and his designs are products of interactions between local climate, urban spaces, society and culture, and they are truly Hong Kong style. Actually, architectural designs in Hong Kong before the 1970's were made with considerations for the relationship between the buildings and the climate, the environment and urban spaces; and thus most residential blocks had balconies and canopies, and office buildings were equipped with tinted or sunshade windows and high ceilings, while designs for schools focused mainly on the harmony of spaces and being green.

投機建築文化
The Culture of Speculative Architecture

　　上世紀八十年代以後，香港經濟起飛，高地價政策、空調的普及化、大地產商的崛起、政府權力的集中，形成了一種非常短視不重視環保、忽略空間的投機建築文化。一式一樣的監獄式設計和中央冷氣大商場，樓要高要大，樓底卻越來越低，公共空間越來越少，思考空間越來越窄。

In the 1980's, the economy of Hong Kong took off, then came the high land price policy, the popularisation of air conditioning, the rise of major developers, the centralisation of power in the government; and eventually a kind of speculative architectural culture without foresight was formed, paying no attention and respect to environmental protection and space. As a result, designs like prisons, which were more or less the same, mushroomed – shopping malls with central air-conditioning sprang up; towers were getting bigger and higher while ceiling heights were getting lower and lower; public spaces became less and less, and spaces for thinking got smaller and smaller.

　　劉秀成可以説是香港建築界的異數，其建築風格繼承了香港上世紀七十年代的優良傳統，不僅重視外表，更強調建築作為與氣候、功能、都市空間和社會文化互動的產物。

Patrick Lau is a variance in the architecture industry of Hong Kong. His architectural style has its heritage from the fine tradition of the 1970's, with a lot of attention paid on the appearance of a building, while stressing the fact that architecture is a product of the interaction between climate, functions, urban spaces, society and culture.

學校與監獄
Schools and Prisons

2002年獲得香港建築師學會頒予獎項的澳洲國際學校呈現出非常典型的劉氏風格。他要處理的仍是香港非常典型的高密度建築面積，首先利用簡單的石屎結構建築，營造不同的空間層次感，並透過不同的窗戶設計和隔光設計，讓陽光空氣和空間成為主角。沒有雲石大堂，沒有玻璃幕牆這些豪華設計，老老實實地營造學習的空間。

In 2002, the Hong Kong Institute of Architects presented Patrick Lau an award for his design for the Australian International School Hong Kong, and that design is very typical of his style. What Patrick Lau had to handle then was the very common issue of densely built-up area. He used very simple concrete structures to create a sense of

香港澳洲國際學校 *Australian International School Hong Kong*

九龍塘的澳洲國際學校由香港大學建築系劉秀成教授設計，2002年獲建築學會頒授獎項。 In 2002, Patrick Lau, Professor of the Department of Architecture at the University of Hong Kong, received the HKIA Medal of the Year for his design of the Australian International School in Kowloon Tong.

美國國際學校 *American International School*

layering and spatial difference, and allowed sunlight, air and space to be the key figures of the architecture through various designs of windows and shading. It is a simple and honest space for learning without luxurious elements like marble lobby or glass curtain wall.

八十年代以後，香港的學校建築，都是以設計監獄的概念來建造，難怪香港教育水平一落千丈。建築設計反映了業主的意識形態和文化水平，硬件和軟件是互動的。劉氏的學校作品，大都是國際學校，業主重視的不是香港政府那種所謂公平公開的官僚程序，而是學生和老師，建築必須以人為本。劉氏的學校建築設計應該是香港學校的典範，造價不高，但富有空間感和重視人性。

Since the 80's, all schools in Hong Kong are constructed based on the concept of prison design, no wonder the standards of education in Hong Kong have plummeted. The architectural design of a building reflects the ideology and cultural level of the owner. Hardware and software should be interactive. The designs of Patrick Lau for schools are mostly for international schools; and what his clients care about are not the so-called fair and open bureaucratic procedures, but students and teachers, and the architectures must be human-based, putting people first. The school designs of Patrick Lau should be the model for all schools in Hong Kong. Their costs are not high, with a strong sense of space, and paying great attention to human nature.

香港的投機資本主義和官僚主義常常把一些不合理的事情合理化，學校建築就是一例。若香港政府能容許像劉氏這樣的建築師參與設計學校，對香港教育質素的提升也大有幫助。

In Hong Kong, speculative capitalism and bureaucracy often rationalise things unreasonable; and school architecture is one example. If only the Hong Kong Government would use architects like Patrick Lau for their designs for schools, the quality of education in Hong Kong would be greatly enhanced.

學校設計的貧乏
Poor School Designs

　　學校設計是一門非常複雜的學問，但香港投資在教育與設計的研究實在少得可憐，2001年香港中文大學建築系設立學校設計研究所是個好開始，要真正產生影響，始終要是讓有質素及經驗的建築師參與具體的設計與研究。早期劉氏的學校建築大多在半山區，加上是國際學校，所以普羅市民並不熟悉他的作品。

School design is like rocket science, very complicated, but in Hong Kong the investment on research on education and related designs is very little. In 2001, the Department of Architecture of Chinese University founded an institute for school design, and that was a good start; but in order to create an impact, good and experienced architects should be invited to involve in the designs and researches. The early works of Patrick Lau in school design are situated mainly in the Mid-Levels, with most of them being international schools; and that is why the general public is not familiar with his works.

　　新建的澳洲國際學校就在九龍塘地鐵站旁邊，人流比較多，從外面也能看見這所學校富有動感和色彩的形態——幾個簡單的陽光設計，顏色的配合，就突出了澳洲人的陽光性格。假如學生、家長、老師和公眾人士有機會參觀劉氏的作品，再比較現時港府的學校建築，必能明白兩者之分別，也會明白為甚麼香港人會爭相讓孩子入讀國際學校，學習環境實在比政府設計的優勝得多。學校是培養創意的場所，其設計也應是顯露創意的產物，而非打壓創意的成果，在香港大學建築系任教的劉秀成相信也必定會同意這個説法。

His latest school design, Australia International School is right next to the Kowloon Tong MTR Station, where a lot of people commute. By simply looking from the outside, one could see that it is a vibrant institute full of colours – highlighting the sunny personality of the Australians with several simple sunlight designs and colour matches. If students, parents, teachers and the public have the opportunity to visit Lau's works and compare them with the schools designed by our government, then they would definitely see the difference, and understand why so many people are so eager to get their children into international schools, since the learning environment of an international school is so much better than that of the local schools. School is a place to develop creativity, and its design should reflect innovation; and not something suppressing creativity. I believe Prof. Patrick Lau, who teachs in the Department of Architecture in University of Hong Kong, would agree with this.

香港澳洲國際學校： 香港九龍九龍塘羅福道3A
Australian International School Hong Kong:
3A Norfolk Road, Kowloon Tong, Kowloon, Hong Kong

建築須照顧天地人
——專訪劉秀成教授

»Architecture with Heaven, Earth and Man in Perfect Harmony

– Interview with Prof. Patrick Lau «

　　香港建築師學會每年頒發的建築年獎是香港唯一具權威性的建築設計獎項，由提名到遴選，都有本地和國際建築師參與。2002年獲得大獎的作品是劉秀成設計的澳洲國際學校。劉秀成任教於香港大學建築系，是香港學校建築的專家，作品大部分都是學校或與教育相關的建築，並多次獲得香港建築師學會的獎項，其中包括法國國際學校。筆者與劉教授進行了一次簡短的訪問，由澳洲國際學校開始，談到香港的學校建築設計，以及香港未來建築發展的路向。

The Hong Kong Institute of Architects Annual Awards are the most prestigious awards for architectural design in Hong Kong, and both local and international architects are involved in the whole process of nomination and selection. In 2002, Patrick Lau received the HKIA Medal of the Year for his design of the Australian International School Hong Kong. Patrick Lau is the Honorary Professor of the Department of Architecture at the University of Hong Kong, and is an outstanding architect and expert in school design. Most of his works are related to schools and education, and he has been awarded by the Hong Kong Institute of Architects for many times, including that for the French International School. I did a brief interview with Prof. Lau on school design in Hong Kong, and we started with his design for the Australian International School, and wrapped up with the future development of Hong Kong architecture.

□胡恩威 Mathias Woo　　■劉秀成 Patrick Lau

香港建築應有中庭
Hong Kong Architecture and Courtyard

□澳洲國際學校的設計有甚麼特點？

□ What are the characteristics of the design for the Australian International School?

■我想先從設計過程開始講起。我和澳洲國際學校合作多年，每次他們搬校舍，我也有協助建築設計方面的工作，所以我對澳洲國際學校的教育理念和方針十分清楚。我覺得設計學校有點像找裁縫做衫，建築師要了解該校的教育理念，教學方法和營運模式，度身訂造，澳洲國際學校的設計概念也是根據校址地形環境和其教育理念發展出來的。

■ I'd like to start with the design process. I have been working with the Australian International School for many years. Every time they moved their school, I assisted in the architectural design work, and thus I am very familiar with their idea, philosophy and principles of education. I think the job for designing a school is like that of a tailor. The architect should have a full understanding of the education philosophy of the school, its teaching methods and model of operation; and then custom make a design for it. The design concept of the Australian International School was developed in this way, based on the site, the terrain and education philosophy of the school.

澳洲是一個喜歡陽光和戶外活動的國家，所以我在整體規劃上盡量利用有限的土地，創造不同大小的戶外空間，如天台的戶外游泳池，足球場，籃球場；建築物設計方面，透過中庭的空間，把陽光和空氣帶到建築物裡面；而在顏色運用方面，以白色為主色，配上澳洲常用的綠色和黃色。我的建築作品最重視天，地，人這三個元素，天是氣候，地是地勢地形和四周環境，人就是建築的用途以及使用者的需要，澳洲國際學校也是根據這套理論發展出來。香港地少人多，其實應更重視地的運用，在香港從事建築設計最重要的就是處理地的問題。

Australia is a country with a lot of sunshine and outdoor activities, and so I tried to create many outdoor spaces of different sizes with the limited land in my overall plan, such as the outdoor swimming pool on the rooftop, the football field and basketball court. Through the atrium, sunshine and fresh air are brought into the building. As for the colour scheme, white is the key colour, with touches of green and yellow, which are synonymous with Australia. The most important elements for my architectural designs are heaven, earth and man. Heaven is the climate; earth is the terrain, topography and the surrounding environment; and man is the function of the building and the needs of the users. The Australian International School was developed with this theory in mind. Hong Kong is a densely populated place where land is scarce, and so people should be very careful in the way they use the land, and the most important job for the people engaged in architectural design in Hong Kong should be to handle the issue of land use.

澳洲國際學校的地皮面積很小，旁邊又是大馬路，首先要處理的是空間的佈局，班房的安排，以及人流（學生移動）空間。我覺得在香港的天氣環境和地少人多的情況下，建築物都應該有中庭，一方面讓陽光可以透到每一個樓層，另一方面更能營造一個通風的環境，減低空調的應用。

The site area for the Australian International school is tight, and there is a main road beside the school. So, the first thing I had to deal with then was the spatial layout – how to arrange the classrooms and the spaces for people (students) flow. I think that with Hong Kong being a small and densely populated city with a hot climate, there should be an atrium in most buildings, so that sunshine could get into each floor, and ventilation would be better, and that would reduce the use of air-conditioning.

☐你對香港的學校建築有甚麼看法？
☐What do you think of the architectural designs of schools in Hong Kong?

　　■由建築署提出的「標準學校」（Standard School）其實是一個不錯的想法，設計成功的話，既可省錢也可以加快興建速度，但缺點就是一錯就影響深遠。香港的標準學校的問題就是不太考慮使用者的需要，不太關注建築物四周的環境，缺乏與當地社區文化氣候的配合。一間學校最重要的部分是入口，學生進入了學校，要知道方向，知道如何在學校移動，因為學校看重的是學生在學校的運作所產生的互動。香港學校的設計者大都以為，把學生集中在班房裡聽老師講課，就是學校最重要的功能。

　　■The idea of the "Standard School" proposed by the Architectural Services Department is quite a good idea. If the design works, it would save money and take less time for construction, but the drawback is that consequences would be profound and long-lasting once there is a mistake. The problem with the standard school design in Hong Kong is the lack of considerations for the users' needs and the environment around, and there is no coordination with the cultural climate of the neighbouring communities. The most important part of a school is the entrance. Once students get into the school, they should be able to tell their direction and know how to move around in the campus because the school is concerned with the interactions created by the activities of its students. Most school designers in Hong Kong think that the most important function of a school is to gather students in the classrooms to listen to their teachers.

　　□是否有點像一所監獄？
　　□ Is it a bit like a prison?

　　■概念上是十分相似的，也許這就是香港教育的問題所在，學生在中小學已經習慣了被動。所以我認為香港應該放棄「標準學校」這個概念，讓不同的建築師和辦學的校長老師發展不同個性的校舍設計，其實我所設計的國際學校的建造費和「標準學校」的差不多，在興建速度上也慢不了多少，好像澳洲國際學校的落成日期，較旁邊的兩間「標準學校」的還要早。

　　■The concept is very similar, and perhaps that is the problem with education in Hong Kong. Primary and secondary students are so used to being passive. That is why I think we should get rid of the idea of the standard school in Hong Kong, and encourage diverse school designs with distinctive personalities by different architects with contribution from school principals and teachers. In fact, the construction time and costs for the international schools I designed are more or less the same as those for the standard school. Let's take the Australian International School for example, it took less time to build than the two adjacent standard schools.

□你怎樣看香港建築的未來發展？
□How do you see the future development of architecture in Hong Kong?

■香港其實擁有很多優秀的建築師，只是客觀條件的局限，讓這些人才不能發揮，政府在這方面應該多做工作，一方面開放不同類型的建築設計工程讓私人執業建築師參與設計工作；同時亦推動市民大眾對建築的認識。
■There are actually a lot of good architects in Hong Kong, but there are also a lot of limitations in the objective conditions, and so these architects could not realise their full potentials. The government should put in more efforts in this area by offering more of their various architectural projects to architects in private practice, allowing these architects to participate in different types of architectural designs, while enhancing the understanding and interest of the public in architecture.

要重視設計水平
Putting More Effort on Architectural Design

長遠來説，香港應該發展成為培育亞太區中國建築師的中心，就像倫敦和紐約。所以香港應設立不同與建築設計和建造科技有關的研究教育機構，培養更多不同種類的建築設計人才。現在香港的建築師花了太多時間去管理工程，應投放更多精力在設計工作上，建築師的競爭力將取決於設計水平和運用科技的素質。所以業主，承建商和建築師要是能更重視設計素質和研究，香港的建築服務才可以在中國市場競爭。

In the long run, Hong Kong should become the training centre of architects in the Asia-Pacific region, like London and New York for the west. We should set up different research and education institutes for architectural design and construction technology to nurture a greater variety of talents for architectural design. Architects in Hong Kong are spending too much time on managing projects. They should put more effort on design since the competitiveness of architects will rely on the quality of their designs and their use of technology. Therefore, property owners, contractors and architects have to double their effort on the quality of design and research in order for Hong Kong to gain some competitiveness in construction services in the market of China.

十元紙幣
»The Ten Dollar Bank Note«

新的香港十元紙幣，十分難看，像玩《大富翁》遊戲的玩具銀紙，像清明時節供奉先人的冥錢：顏色過深，圖案太花，也沒有甚麼特色，是一張設計得不好的「歐洲風格」紙幣，十分小家子氣。

The new ten-dollar bill of Hong Kong looks quite hideous. It seems like the toy money in Monopoly, or paper money for offerings for the dead. The colour is too deep and patterns too chaotic, and it has no character at all. It is a poorly designed "European style" bank note, very petty.

舊香港紙幣的設計，已經建立了自己的風格和特色，要改革就必須突破，要變得更好而不是更差。香港政府是設計盲，以為官大就懂設計，自把自為，以為光顧一些國際設計顧問，就保證有好的設計。官方不明白，好的設計最重要的是顧問，也要懂得尊重設計、具有設計知識。

The design of the old bank notes of Hong Kong has already established its own style and character; should there be a change, it has to be a breakthrough, to transform the notes into something better and not worse. The government of Hong Kong is illiterate in design. There are officials who think they would understand design if their positions are high enough, who think if they hire some international consultants, that would guarantee a good design. They don't understand, a good design needs a good consultant, who respects design and possesses the knowledge and ability on design.

飛龍標記（按：香港政府花了九百萬港幣聘請國際顧問設計）是一次錯誤，十元紙幣是另一次。錯誤其實天天在發生，最差是政府官員的態度，不好好學習他國政府處理設計的政策。

The "flying dragon" logo was a mistake (designed by an international consultancy firm hired by the government with nine million HKD), now the ten-dollar bill is once again a big mistake. These mistakes are in fact happening all the time, and the biggest problem is the official's attitude, and they would not learn from other overseas governments on policies regarding design.

　　新加坡政府比香港專業，十分重視公共建築的設計的策劃和管理，常派官員出國進修和參與國際研討會，學習歐美日等設計先進國的政府設計政策。香港要發展創意工業，首要是政府要改變現在的反智設計政策，改善政府的設計遴選機制，並盡量以外判形式供香港的私人執業設計和建築設計者參與，避免閉門造車。

The government of Singapore is more professional than that of Hong Kong, and they place great importance on design, coordination and management of public architecture. They would also send government officials abroad to study and participate in international conferences, to learn from other places like Europe, America or Japan which are more advanced on design. Hong Kong would like to develop its creative industries, the top mission in the priority list should be to reform the current anti-intelligence design policy, to improve on the system of selection on design, and to outsource projects to private designers and architects in order to avoid the issue of carrying out projects without reference to what the world needs.

　　現在政府各部門的標記設計都十分差勁，運輸署是典型例子，一方面是幾年來改了兩次，越改越怪相，這種不尊重設計的態度是把香港提升為國際城市的絆腳石。香港政府應該有自知之明，要明白政府官員不是萬能的。

Logos of various government departments are designed quite poorly. A classical example would be that of The Transport Department, it has been re-designed twice in the last few years, the newer edition is even worse. This attitude of disrespect on design will become an obstacle for Hong Kong to become an international city. Government officials of Hong Kong should know themselves better; they should understand that being a government official does not mean he or she would know it all.

　　歐盟的歐羅紙幣設計以建築為主題，四平八穩，屬經典式的設計。昔日的法國法郎紙幣設計得十分浪漫，都是以藝術文化人物為主題，最為可愛的是以《小王子》故事人物為設計主題的。香港的新十元紙幣根本沒有任何主題，只是大堆凌亂的線條，最令人費解的是那條莫名其妙的絲帶和過分細小的簽名，第一次看見，還以為是某某飲食集團的贈券。

The bank note of the European Union is themed in architecture, a solid and classic design. The old Franc bank note of France was very romantic, with the theme of each note carrying an important artistic/cultural figure, the most adorable one has to be the 50F bill designed with the figure of Le Petit Prince. There is not any theme on the new ten-dollar bill of Hong Kong, just strands of chaotic lines. What puzzles people most would be that curious ribbon and tiny signatures. At first sight, the new bank note could very well be mistaken as a coupon of some restaurant.

藝術是一門學問
»Art Is A Science«

　　香港人對藝術有很多偏見，原因是絕大部分的香港人都不清楚藝術是怎樣的一回事。香港的教育制度欠缺健全和合理的藝術教育課程，香港人從小到大都沒有深入認識藝術的機會，繼而造成香港大眾媒體對藝術總存在着一種歧視。

People in Hong Kong have a lot of bias in the way they look at art. The reason is that most of them do not understand what art is. The education system in Hong Kong lacks a sound and rational curriculum in arts education. Growing up in Hong Kong, children do not have the opportunity to gain a solid understanding of art. For that reason, there exists a sense of discrimination against art from the mass media in Hong Kong.

　　其實藝術和生活息息相關，我們穿的衣服，看電影、電視，讀書睇雜誌，聽音樂看漫畫，家居的設計……天天接觸的事物，都是藝術衍生出來的產物，藝術本身是一門學問，一種知識。

In fact, art is closely related to our lives. The clothes we wear, the television and films we watch, books and magazines we read, as well as music, comics, home furnishing... things that we are in touch with everyday are all products of art. Art itself is a science.

　　所謂美與不美，除了是主觀感以外，更重要的是客觀的知性分析。像八大山人和畢加索畫，都可以用藝術知識的角度來理解。有些香港人愛說藝術是主觀的，沒有標準。簡直一派胡言，態度反智。若藝術真的是「主觀」的話，便不需要在大學設立藝術系了，也不需要建藝術博物館了。藝術能夠成為一門學科，因為它是人類發展出來的一種知識系統，也是人類精神文明和健康的基礎。

Other than subjective feelings, what is more important is objective and intellectual analysis when aesthetics is concerned. For example, the paintings of Bada Shanren (a leading painter of the Ming

Dynasty) and Picasso can be appreciated through an aesthetic point of view. Many in Hong Kong like to say that art is subjective and without objective standards, that is complete nonsense and anti-intelligence! Should art be really "subjective", then there wouldn't be the need of any Arts Department in universities, nor would there be the need for art museums anymore. Art became an academic subject because it is a knowledge system, which is also the basis of humanities and spiritual health.

一般香港人過分功利，只重視即時效果，總覺得藝術可有可無。他們不明白，語文能力要好，最主要是學好文學而不是單純的文法；香港人要有「創意」，先要對藝術建立深入的認識，才能培養出具「深度」的創意。藝術和創意不是香港人眼中的「胡來」或隨意發揮，工業和知識型社會十分重視藝術，視藝術為一切發明和創造的根源，像平治房車的設計，就是一種藝術的創造，像新力的影音電子產品是建基於其創造力、想像力的嚴謹設計概念上。

Generally, people living in Hong Kong are utilitarians, who care only about immediate effects and would consider art as dispensable. They do not understand why one should want to improve language skills; why emphasis should be placed on literature and not solely on grammar. Should Hong Kong people want to have "creativity", they would need to establish a thorough understanding of art to cultivate creativity with profundity. Art and creativity are not "random strokes" or free-flow as seen by the eyes of Hong Kong people. Industrial and intellectual societies value arts, seeing arts as the source of all inventiveness and creativity. For example, the design of a Mercedes Benz is a creation of art, and the electronic products by Sony are made with strict design concepts with creativity and imagination as roots.

香港人的創造力通常都是一些小聰明，但也就只限於小聰明。香港人的強項是行政的效率，而不是知識的創造。注重行政效率的香港政府制定的文化藝術政策，就不會從藝術的角度看待藝術。香港的藝術被政府管死了，而香港的商界大部分都視藝術為宣傳工具、裝飾品，都沒有好奇心和興趣去深入認識它。

The creativity of Hong Kong is usually a kind of trivial cleverness, and this sort of minor cleverness is all there is. The strength of Hong Kong people is executive efficiency, and not creation by knowledge. The arts and cultural policies set by the government of Hong Kong focus on executive efficiency, and would not consider art from the point of view of art. In Hong Kong, art is strangled by the regulations of our government. The majority of the commercial sector considers art as promotional tools or decorations. No one has the curiosity and interest to understand it in depth.

香港風格

Hong Kong Style

作者：胡恩威
視覺設計：劉思
攝影：胡恩威、冼嘉弘、張偉樂、林永安
編輯：梁冠麗、徐沛筠
英文翻譯：姚凱琳、梁惠琪
英文校對：梁惠琪
中文校對：胡㮾明

Written by Mathias Woo
Designed by Liu Si
Photos by Mathias Woo, Keith Hiro,
            Cheung Wai Lok and Lam Wing On
Edited by Theresa Leung and Pamela Tsui
English Translation by Melody Yiu, Vicky Leong
English Proofreading by Vicky Leong
Chinese Proofreading by Ming Woo

出版：進念·二十面體 E+E
通訊地址：香港柴灣祥利街 9 號
　　　　　祥利工業大廈 7 樓 B 座
電話：+852-2893-8704
傳真：+852-2838-7527
電郵：info@zuni.org.hk
網址：www.zuni.org.hk

Publisher: Zuni Icosahedron E+E
Address: Unit B, 7/F Cheung Lee Industrial
Building, 9 Cheung Lee Street, Chai Wan,
Hong Kong
Tel: +852-2893-8704
Fax: +852-2838-7527
Email: info@zuni.org.hk
Website: www.zuni.org.hk

發行：城邦（香港）出版集團有限公司

Publishing: CITE(HK) PUBLISHING GROUP
LIMITED
Published in Hong Kong
First Edition, July 2012
ISBN: 978-988-15266-1-8
All Rights Reserved

二零一二年七月初版於香港

ISBN: 978-988-15266-1-8
版權所有　翻印必究

印刷：奇傳媒體印刷有限公司
地址：香港油塘高輝道15號萬年工業大廈2樓

Printer: KATCH MEDIA PRINTING LIMITED
Address: 2/F, Long Life Industrial Building,
15 Ko Fai Road, Yau Tong,
Kowloon, Hong Kong

進念·二十面體由香港特別行政區政府資助

Zuni Icosahedron is financially supported by
the Government of the Hong Kong Special
Administrative Region